BATH MASSACRE

BATH MASSACRE

AMERICA'S FIRST SCHOOL BOMBING

Arnie Bernstein

THE UNIVERSITY OF MICHIGAN PRESS   ANN ARBOR

Copyright © 2009 by Arnie Bernstein
All rights reserved
Published in the United States of America by
The University of Michigan Press
Manufactured in the United States of America
⊗ Printed on acid-free paper

2012   2011   2010   2009   4   3

A CIP catalog record for this book is available from the British Library.

Library of Congress Cataloging-in-Publication Data

Bernstein, Arnie.
    Bath massacre : America's first school bombing / Arnie Bernstein.
       p.   cm.
    Includes bibliographical references.
    ISBN-13: 978-0-472-11606-5 (cloth : alk. paper)
    ISBN-10: 0-472-11606-1 (cloth : alk. paper)
    ISBN-13: 978-0-472-03346-1 (pbk. : alk. paper)
    ISBN-10: 0-472-03346-8 (pbk. : alk. paper)
    1. Bombings—Michigan—Bath (Township)—History—20th century.
    2. Bath (Mich. : Township)—History—20th century.   3. Students—Crimes
    against—Michigan—Bath (Township)—History—20th century.
    4. Murder—Michigan—Bath (Township)—History—20th century.
    5. Suicide bombers—Michigan—Bath (Township)—History—20th century.
    6. Kehoe, Andrew P. (Andrew Philip), 1872–1927. I. Title.
    F574.B18B47   2009
    977.4'041—dc22   2008048155

    ISBN 978-0-472-02470-4 (electronic)

For the children of Bath

CONTENTS

A voice is heard in Ramah
   lamentation and bitter weeping
Rachel is weeping for her children;
   she refuses to be comforted for her children,
because they are not.

—JEREMIAH 31:15

When lilacs are in bloom
I think of the Bath School explosion
because that day
the children brought bouquets to their teacher

—MARTHA HORTON
SURVIVOR

PROLOGUE: APRIL 16, 2007

The morning of April 16, 2007, dawned clear and bright over central Michigan. In Dewitt, a small town about twenty miles from the state capital of Lansing, ninety-six-year-old Willis Cressman woke at his usual time, ate breakfast, then puttered around the house. A lifelong resident of the area, Cressman lived a good long life. Born in 1911, he'd grown up in the nearby town of Bath. Before retiring, he was a jack-of-all-trades. In various phases of life, he'd worked on road crews, farmed, and operated an excavation business. A veteran of World War II, he was one of the many brave soldiers who hit Anzio Beach on January 22, 1944. He never forgot that day and all the shells exploding around him. Yet Anzio wasn't the first time Cressman was in the midst of deadly explosions.[1]

In her home on the outskirts of nearby Bath, not far from Dewitt, Josephine Cushman Vail, a woman just a few months shy of her ninety-fourth birthday, was beginning her morning as well. Vail and Cressman were old schoolmates, first as students in a one-room schoolhouse during the 1910s and then in a larger, consolidated school in the 1920s. Those days held fond memories of classroom accomplishments, athletic and social events, friends, and a sense of community.[2]

Cressman and Vail had other recollections of the Bath Consolidated

School: the events that unfolded on May 18, 1927. That day was something they never wanted anyone else to experience.

About the time Cressman and Vail began their mornings, Seung-Hui Cho, a twenty-three-year-old student at Virginia Tech, located in Blacksburg, Virginia, started his day. At 7:15 a.m., he entered West Ambler Johnston Hall, an on-campus dormitory, barged into the room of Emily Hilscher, a nineteen-year-old freshman, then shot her and twenty-two-year-old senior Ryan C. Clark, the resident adviser for the floor, who happened to be in Hilscher's room. Both were dead at the scene.

Cho returned to his room in another dorm, changed clothes, deleted his campus e-mail, and removed the hard drive from his computer. As he walked through campus, another student saw Cho hurl what looked like a hard drive and a mobile phone into a pond.

Just before nine, one hour and forty-five minutes after murdering Hilscher and Clark, Cho went to the local post office to mail a package addressed to NBC News in New York City. He was lugging a hefty backpack filled with chains and locks, a knife and hammer, and two pistols. Cho had also stowed nineteen ten- and fifteen-round magazines and nearly four hundred bullets in the backpack.

He returned to campus and entered Norris Hall, where several classrooms and the university's Engineering Science and Mechanics program were located. Cho methodically removed the chains and locks from his backpack and fastened them to the building's three main doors, effectively cutting off any attempt to enter or exit Norris. Once the entranceways were sealed tight, Cho left a note. It said any attempt to break the chains would result in an explosion.

Cho walked up to the second floor, then poked his head inside a classroom. One person who saw him, Erin Sheehan, believed Cho was a student who didn't know what room his class was in. Strange, Sheehan thought, that someone should be lost on campus so late in the semester.

Downstairs a faculty member discovered Cho's handiwork on the doors. He read the note. Although he didn't know about the earlier shootings, the teacher instantly realized something terrible was unfolding at Virginia Tech.

Cho entered room 206 and unleashed his firepower. The shooting spree continued in rooms 207, 204, and 211. There was gunfire. Screams. Students fleeing, knocking into each other, desperate. Blood, bodies, and bullet shells littered the classrooms. In just nine minutes, Cho fired at least 174 rounds.

He then pointed one of the guns at his head and pulled the trigger.

The package he sent to NBC contained a videotape prepared a few weeks earlier. It was Cho's last message to the world. Killers, he declared, are made, forced into desperate acts by others, not born.

The news of the Virginia Tech massacre quickly spread. Cable stations broke into regular coverage, filling television screens across the country with stumbling facts, scraps of information, and some speculation as to what was going on at Virginia Tech. In total, Cho murdered twenty-seven students and five teachers before killing himself.[3]

His actions were declared one of the worst acts of school violence in recent years. It was bigger than the shootings at Columbine High School in Colorado, where two students killed twelve peers, one teacher, and themselves.

In Dewitt, Cressman felt something ache deep inside his soul.[4] Vail's thoughts turned to her long-dead sibling, Ralph. Had he lived, her baby brother would now be eighty-seven years old.[5]

Across the nation people shook their heads and wondered what was becoming of their country. Since the Columbine shootings of April 20, 1999 (almost eight years to the day), there had been unease about safety in schools. Just six months earlier a disturbed individual walked into an Amish one-room schoolhouse in rural Pennsylvania, murdered five little girls, and shot himself. That same week there were school shootings at Platte Canyon High School in Bailey, Colorado, and Weston High School in Cazenovia, Wisconsin. Virginia Tech was the twenty-fifth school shooting in the United States since 2006.[6]

Comparisons between Virginia Tech and Columbine were inevitable. These horrors were described as the two deadliest school shootings in American history.

There was a minor footnote to some news stories about the Virginia Tech massacre. Newspapers, Internet sites, and television reports provided painfully long lists of the "worst school massacres." At the bottom of these rolls was a brief mention of a 1927 incident at a school in Bath, Michigan.

To Cressman and Vail, Virginia Tech replayed a pattern so terribly familiar. A carefully laid out plan. The mailing of a package. A mass killing of students. A spectacular suicide. Here it was April 2007, yet the scenario was so similar.

It was like what William Faulkner once wrote about history, that the past isn't dead. It isn't even the past. Cho was merely repeating something Cressman and Vail had borne witness to decades before. On May 18, 2007, just a month away, it would be eighty years since the "incident" now considered a footnote. Cressman and Vail were survivors of that day, the first school massacre in modern American history.

◆ ◆ ◆

At first glance, Cressman and Vail's childhood home of Bath, Michigan, looks like a place where nothing bad could happen. Located about twelve miles from the state capital of Lansing, Bath has that All-American feeling to it—a quintessential small town steeped in good midwestern values. Bath itself has physically changed over the years, but its essential character has prevailed throughout the decades. In the spring it is alive with green. The town was founded as a farming community with corn and soybeans being the major crops. Sugar beets, which dwindled in popularity through the years, are making a comeback. There's also a dairy farm in the area, home to a large herd of Holsteins. In recent years farmlands have been transformed into housing subdivisions and condominium complexes. The old Kehoe place, west of the town center, was at one point being developed for condos, though these plans fell through. The land ceased to be a farm in 1927 and lay fallow for years. No one wanted to touch it.

There are two main roads in Bath, Webster and Clark (formerly known as Gunnisonville), which intersect at the town's center. An elementary school and middle school are located near the crossroads; the high school is a short walk from these facilities. Schools in the Bath region were originally old-fashioned one-room schoolhouses. In 1922 the district school system brought together this diffuse network in a single building for kindergartners through high school seniors. Today's trio of school buildings was constructed in the post–World War II years after the James Couzens Agricultural School—originally dedicated in 1928 and named after the senator who helped fund the building—finally outlived its usefulness.

Across the street from the elementary and middle schools is a public park built on the site of the old school. The James Couzens Memorial Park is sort of a community catchall. It's a wonderful place to relax, play with the kids, read a book, walk the dog.

At the center of the park is a white wooden tower, the original cupola

Fig. 1. Couzens Memorial Park. *(Photograph by the author.)*

from the roof of the Bath Consolidated School. It rises from the greens with sad elegance, a wooden vestige of what once stood on this land. A sign posted on the cupola tells the structure's history. At the foot of the cupola is a brick pathway with names etched into forty-two of the stones—many of them Cressman's and Vail's childhood friends. Vail's kid brother, "Ralph A. Cushman," is honored with a brick. Just beyond this is a marker, erected by the state of Michigan in 1992, explaining the park's significance. Kitty-corner from this marker is a boulder with a large plaque bolted to the stone face. The plaque lists the names of thirty-eight children and four adults. The names of two other adults are conspicuous by their absence.

South of the park is more greenery, the grounds and trees of Pleasant Hill Cemetery. The graveyard dates back to the late nineteenth century and pretty much everyone in town is related to someone buried there. Mothers and fathers, daughters and sons, grandparents and grandchildren—generations bound by silence—rest together under family headstones. Pleasant Hill is well named. Its meditative stillness is broken only by the occasional sound of a passing car, the call of birds, or the noise of children wafting along the wind from the schools down Webster Road.

Wandering through the cemetery one sees a pattern emerging from the headstones. Emilie Marian Bromandt, 1916–1927. Robert F. Bromandt, 1914–1927. Floyd E. Burnett, 1914–1927. Russell J. Chapman, 1918–1927. Ralph A. Cushman, 1919–1927. Katherine Foote, 1916–1927. Galen Lyle Harte, 1914–1927. LaVere Robert Harte, 1917–1927. Stanley Harte, 1915–1927. Doris Elaine Johns, 1918–1927. James Emerson Medcoff, 1918–1927. Emma Nickols, 1914–1927. Richard Dibble Richardson, 1914–1927. Pauline M. Shirts, 1916–1927. Harold LeMoyne Woodman, 1918–1927. They are scattered like delicate leaves throughout the cemetery, these headstones of children, all sharing the 1927 date. These childhoods, so abruptly ended, still whisper through Bath like the muted song of a mournful choir.

May 18, 1927, started out as a perfect spring day, the air freshly scrubbed by the night's rain and fragrant with flowers. Within a few hours the smell of lilacs in bloom was overtaken by the stench of smoke and dynamite, flame and blood. The north wing of the Bath Consolidated School was in ruins, destroyed from beneath by carefully planted explosives. A second blast left the hulking remains of a Ford truck at the school entrance. Thirty-six children and two teachers died in the initial blast; the Ford explosion killed two adult bystanders and another child, as well as the school superintendent. One child hung on for three months before dying from her injuries. Fifty-eight children and adults were injured.

To the west of the school, a farmhouse and surrounding buildings on the property were reduced to smoking embers. The next day, tied to a cart near the henhouse, authorities found the charred remains of a body, too badly burned to determine its gender but assumed by the overall circumstances to be a woman. A stenciled sign posted on a fence at the edge of the farm read "Criminals Are Made, Not Born."

Another man died when the Ford truck exploded. He was the owner of the burned farm. His final moments of life were a spectacular act of murder-suicide that capped his destruction of the school and farm. Andrew P. Kehoe was the dead man's name, and everyone in Bath knew who he was.

Chapter 1

A COMMUNITY IN MICHIGAN

One idea leads to another. The Northwest Ordinance of 1787 was a bold step in the development of the American landscape. Entire areas of wilderness, filled with miles upon miles of uncut forest, home to pristine rivers, teeming with wildlife and mysterious indigenous peoples—popularly known as Indians—filled this rugged new world. To the north, sharing a border with Canada, were enormous lakes, sources of freshwater that offered late 1700s populations a powerful natural resource.

The ordinance divvied up these virgin lands into what were known as "township areas," some of which amounted to a few acres, others the size of entire states.[1] Eleven years later, the Continental Congress set in motion laws that allowed sale of these northwestern lands, ultimately beginning what was known as Manifest Destiny, the God-given right of the United States to control and expand into the continent of North America from the Atlantic to the Pacific Oceans. The lands feeding off the Great Lakes in the north were particularly favorable to early pioneers. With their untold resources, these regions were ideal places for development. The territory of Michigan was established in 1805, and with the completion of the Erie Canal in 1825 white settlers came in droves.

On March 2, 1831, a part of the territory was declared to be Clinton

County, named after Dewitt Clinton, the governor of New York.[2] It was an exemplary spot to begin life in this world. In 1836, Ira Cushman, a New York resident with roots that stretched back to the *Mayflower,* settled in Clinton County. He built a log cabin, raised corn, potatoes, and wheat, then sent for his father and brothers. Cushman's descendants would prosper throughout Clinton County well into the next century.[3]

More pioneers—of English, Irish, Scottish, and German extraction—soon followed. Silas Rose, another New Yorker, came in 1837.[4] With his wife and five children, three teams of oxen, two cows, and a powerful desire to farm the land, Rose carved out a section of woods as his family's homestead. He named the area Bath in honor of his hometown in New York state, a town that itself was named after the ancient city of Roman baths in central England.[5]

The first schoolhouse, a simple one-room affair, was founded in 1840 to accommodate the dozen or so children of the area.[6] Clinton County was gradually subdivided into townships; Bath Township was officially founded in the spring of 1843 with its first election held on April 18.[7]

Expansion continued. The 1860 census showed 515 people living in the area, the majority of them farmers.[8] More one-room schoolhouses emerged to accommodate the children of the growing farming population. The sons of Bath joined the fight for the Union during the Civil War. A Baptist church was founded in 1868, the Methodist congregation in 1869.[9]

A sawmill and a brick factory followed. They provided the grist for more building. At the beginning of the twentieth century, Bath was a flourishing village and the center of a growing township. Businesses lined the small streets, providing everything a farming community could ask for: food, supplies, and a post office. As the railroad pushed its way across the country to the Pacific coast, the town built a train depot.[10] With the depot came something one wouldn't expect in such a small burg: a hotel. It made an excellent way station for travelers in need of a hot meal and simple room for the night.

What Bath Township lacked was a central school system.

Small schoolhouses still dotted the region. Students, ranging from kindergarten to high school seniors, learned together under the confines of one roof in one room. As the area grew, the township divided the map into school districts. Fractional schools were built so neighboring school districts could be served by a single facility.[11] For the time being, this satisfied the needs of the region. The school year was based on the agrarian calendar. Students attended classes from fall (the end of the harvest season) to spring (the beginning of the planting season). Summers were reserved for the growing season, when every hand was needed on the family farm. Children learned farming basics: chores; milking cows; shearing sheep; and planting, nurturing, and harvesting crops.

While Bath remained a quiet, though steadily growing community, its placement in the hinterlands of Michigan kept it out of step with much of what was going on in the more industrialized parts of the country. After much experimentation, Thomas Edison, the inventor known as "The Wizard of Menlo Park," used his New Jersey laboratory to create a system wherein the power of controlled electricity could be channeled through wires into his new invention: the light bulb. From there his experiments grew in scope and impact. By 1882, New York City had the first electric power plant in the United States, providing energy at the flick of a switch for fifty-nine customers. Within a few years, such plants were springing up across urban areas throughout the world, providing a cheap and safe form of power to millions. Electric lights shone on Americans from coast-to-coast, spread throughout European capitals, and into vast Mother Russia.[12]

Yet Bath, like so many rural areas across the United States, remained without this new power. Local sawmills, so vital to building in the region, continued to rely on steam-based power. The steam engine was a mobile creature. It could be used for lumbering in wooded areas or to run farm machinery such as tractors and heavy-duty equipment to construct homes or raise a barn.[13]

Another basic source of power—farm animals—was a Bath staple. Oxen were used for plowing; eventually the heavy-muscled and thick-brained creatures gave way to sleeker models in the form of horses. Horses moved faster, which certainly improved the speed of farm work. They also offered more options for transportation; rather than using a slow-moving animal to pull a cart to town, people had the choice of a team of horses or riding a solo mount—something a farmer wouldn't dream of doing with an ox.[14]

In 1907 Fred Glass, the local druggist, assembled *The Pocket Directory of Bath, Michigan*. The booklet provided readers with a list of businesses vital to the local economy. Many of the enterprises served multiple roles. The local grocery store sold dry goods along with "Men's and Ladies' Furnishings and Working Garments." James Sweeney, a notary public, wore several hats with interests in money lending, real estate, and insurance. There were a few blacksmiths available for repairing wood and iron machinery or shoeing horses. The directory read like a utopian lay-out for the tiny community. An advertisement for A. B. Klooz's hardware store summed up the general feeling about area commerce.

> So bring me your hardware troubles
>> To me they are but joys;
> And they will disappear like soapsuds bubbles
>> You blew when girls and boys—

As the twentieth century marched forward, a grain elevator towered majestically over downtown. A stockyard and hatchery provided new ser-vices for people used to basic butchering on their own farms. The first town bank was opened in 1910.[15]

To the east lay Detroit, where Henry Ford pioneered a new form of transportation: the automobile. These gasoline-powered machines promised to bring a faster, more efficient form of mobility to the bur-geoning community. By the mid-1910s, automobiles and trucks regularly traversed the dusty roads crisscrossing Bath. Although it had no central source of electricity, Bath was thriving as a model of a small-town modern community.[16]

◆ ◆ ◆

On June 28, 1914, far away from Bath in Sarajevo, Bosnia-Herzegovina, a Yugoslav nationalist named Gavrilo Princip fired a gun, killing Arch-duke Franz Ferdinand, heir to the Austro-Hungarian throne. This assas-sination set off a series of events that led to war among European na-tions. It was a truly modern war. Trenches, dug as protection for soldiers, lined the continent. Countryside regions turned into bloody and scarred battlefields. Another modern invention, the airplane, dropped bombs and fired bullets from the sky. Dynamite blew up land and men. Pyrotol served the same deadly purpose as dynamite.

Dynamite—ignitable tubes developed in the 1860s by the Swedish chemist Alfred Nobel—was made up of three parts nitroglycerin, one part diatomaceous earth, and a small admixture of sodium carbonate. It had tremendous power to destroy, saving time and labor in construction and providing an effective weapon during wartime.[17] Pyrotol, an alterna-tive to dynamite used extensively on the fields of battle, was a smokeless but potent mixture of nitroglycerin, guncotton, and petrolatum. The chemicals were dissolved in acetone, dried, then forced through a die to make thin brown cords.[18]

The United States was neutral but kept a wary eye on Europe as the Great War raged on. On May 17, 1915, a German submarine torpedoed the *Lusitania,* a British luxury liner. In just eighteen minutes the mighty ship was gone, killing 1,198 of the passengers on board, 128 of whom were Americans, sparking outrage among citizens throughout the country. Still President Woodrow Wilson maintained neutrality, a position that did not last long. The Germans grew bolder, taking out American merchant vessels carrying munitions and other supplies to Great Britain. Finally, on April 6, 1917, the United States joined the Allied forces in the fight. The battle raged for another year, but the Allies valiantly held on to victory. Cease-fire came at 11:00 a.m. on November 11, 1918—the eleventh hour of the eleventh day of the eleventh month. Celebrations sprang up throughout towns large and small around the globe.

The revelry extended to Bath, which had seen its share of sons volunteer—and in some cases make the ultimate sacrifice—for the "War to End All Wars." Willis Cressman, then a child of seven, joined his family and neighbors in the festivities. He held his ears as people enthusiastically celebrated by setting off dynamite in the streets.[19]

Chapter 2

ANDREW P. KEHOE

Some remembered him being quite friendly to children.

"He was the nicest man," recalled one survivor. If he was at the school when children arrived in the morning, he would always smile and say hello.[1] A neighbor swore that "he never saw a saner man" than Kehoe.[2] Another survivor remembered that as Kehoe drove up on his way to the school on the morning of May 18 he tipped his hat to her. Kehoe waited politely until she crossed the street, then resumed the drive toward his target.[3]

Just who was Andrew P. Kehoe? A benevolent man who cared about youngsters? Never a saner man? A gentleman to a little girl as he drove toward destruction? "The world's worst demon,"[4] (as one writer dubbed him), for planning the bombing of a schoolhouse full of children?

The truth is he was all of these things.

Kehoe's life story is a series of remnants vaguely documented and filtered through the horror of his crimes. His father, Philip Kehoe, was an Irish Catholic immigrant, one of many who left the Emerald Isle in the wake of the 1840s potato famine. Upon arriving in the United States, Philip, his six brothers, and their parents settled in Maryland. When expansion seized the American consciousness, Philip was one of many immigrants who joined the native-born looking to the country's western lands. He headed to the growing Michigan Territory and bought some farmland near Tecumseh, one of the first three settlements in the territory,[5] located just north of the Michigan-Ohio border. The region was largely populated by farmers.

Once he was established, Philip Kehoe was joined by his brothers and parents. Tecumseh was seemingly a second homeland for immigrants such as the Kehoe clan; the area was largely settled by Irish natives. In time, Kehoe built up a successful farm where he raised both crops and cattle.[6]

Philip wed Mary Malone, whose background—having been raised by an Irish Catholic priest—was similar to Kehoe's. Their first child, a daughter, was born in 1860, and a second child arrived in 1862. The birth probably had complications, for Mary was dead about a week after the infant was born. Philip soon remarried another Irish Catholic émigré, Mary McGovern, whose family came to the area from New York state. Between 1862 and 1870, the couple had four daughters. On February 1, 1872, the first son, Andrew Philip Kehoe, was born.[7] Two more daughters and another son followed shortly.

Andrew fulfilled the Old World sense of primogeniture, an Irish son finally arriving after a brood of daughters. Though the Kehoe household was enormous, their home was rather small, a simple farmhouse overflowing with children. Like his sisters before him, Andrew began his education at the Culbertson School, a small building not far from home.[8]

Andrew learned basic skills of reading, mathematics, and geography at Culbertson. Outside of school, he developed a fascination with electricity the way other children might have indulged in sports. Philip's farm became a giant laboratory for Andrew. He regularly toyed with new ideas for improving farm production through the use of crude electric-powered gizmos.[9] One neighbor was amazed by the contraptions used on the Kehoe farm, machinery probably devised by the creative boy.[10] Andrew also developed a proclivity for being alone, lost in his thoughts, isolated and inward in spirit from his older and younger siblings.

Philip Kehoe was a community stalwart on several fronts, a larger than life figure who held minor elective offices in the region. Though a staunch Democrat, he managed to succeed in a largely Republican area.[11] A deeply religious man, Philip was an influential member of a Catholic parish located in nearby Clinton.[12] The elder Kehoe's religious beliefs certainly spread to his children; one Kehoe daughter eventually entered a convent.[13]

He was also active in local organizations that served as venues for social outings to rural populations. These groups provided an opportunity to voice opinions and learn more about factors influencing their lives. Philip zealously participated in these meetings, using them as a platform to expound on his theories of farming. He was of the mind that the farmer should be in control of his own destiny and engaged in heated discussions with his peers on ways to oversee every aspect of production, from raising crops to setting prices. Kehoe firmly believed that by withholding crops from the market, farmers could maintain financial control over their product.[14] It is quite probable that Andrew attended some of these meetings; certainly Philip Kehoe's philosophies stayed with and influenced Andrew after he acquired his own farm in Bath.

Other issues raised at these salons focused on taxation. Again, Philip made his thoughts clear to anyone within earshot. He insisted there be firm oversight of public funds. If the people's money was being spent on local government, utilities, and schools, then, by God, the people must control how these entities were run. Once more, Philip's strong fiscal ideas made an indelible imprint on his son.

As Andrew approached age ten, there was a noticeable change in his mother. Mary was often ill, and her energy level simply couldn't keep up with the large Kehoe clan. It was "a disease of the nervous system" that afflicted her, a condition that slowly and painfully drained physical abilities. Throughout Andrew's teen years, Mary was confined to bed, the beginning of a decade-long decline.[15] As he completed school, Andrew grew involved in local activities. He often participated in community theater productions and earned favorable reviews in one newspaper.[16]

By the time Andrew turned eighteen, his mother's condition had reduced her to complete paralysis. On November 5, 1890, Mary McGovern Kehoe finally succumbed.[17]

After her death Philip Kehoe, some sixty years old and suffering from arthritis, married once again. His new wife, Frances Wilder, was—like Philip—a widowed single parent raising several children. She was considerably younger than Philip, yet an older man taking on a "child bride" was not uncommon for the times. With his life taking a new direction, Philip Kehoe built a sturdy brick home near his wooden farmhouse for the new Mrs. Kehoe.[18] Frances and Andrew—who was three years older

than his father's new wife—developed a mutual loathing, which ultimately led the son to depart from his father's home.[19]

Kehoe's life grows murky at this point. It's thought that he enrolled at
Michigan State College (later Michigan State University) in East Lansing, where he briefly studied the burgeoning trade of electrical engineering. As a student, one would think he showed the same aptitude for
working with electricity that he displayed as a child.[20] A man who knew
how to harness this force had unlimited potential. Andrew Kehoe was
one of many modern Prometheuses, tempting the electrical Zeus as he
learned to conquer the new fire. Undoubtedly Andrew knew the dangers
involved in harnessing this raw energy that could sneak through wires to
cause serious damage or death.

At some point Kehoe headed south to Missouri, where he studied
electrical engineering at a Saint Louis school. Not much is known about
his time in Saint Louis, one of the many missing pieces in the Kehoe
enigma. In the days following the Bath blast, one of his sisters-in-law revealed that sometime during his Saint Louis years Kehoe was knocked
unconscious.[21] Whether it was a jolt of electricity or perhaps falling off a
ladder she couldn't say. But for two weeks Kehoe lay in a coma, floating
in and out of consciousness. The big question, of course, is did this accident damage Kehoe's brain to the point where his psyche was permanently seared? This is an intangible that simply cannot be answered.
Clearly something happened when Kehoe was knocked out, for it was
enough to put him in the two-week coma.[22]

After recovering, Kehoe returned to his electrical passions. For a time
he worked in Saint Louis, then drifted throughout the Midwest honing
his electrical knowledge. At some point he headed north to Iowa where
he found employment as a lineman. He returned to Michigan in 1905,
the dawn of the new century.[23]

◆ ◆ ◆

Life at Philip Kehoe's household had changed considerably. There was a
new Kehoe child, three-year-old Irene. Although his relations with
Philip's new family were still strained, Andrew Kehoe moved into his
childhood home and resumed working Philip's land.[24]

Like many farmers, Andrew cleared his father's fields of old tree
stumps and inconveniently placed boulders. He turned to the resource
commonly used for this purpose: dynamite and war surplus pyrotol.

Over time Kehoe's resentment toward his father's new family developed into detestment. The first son, seemingly poised to inherit his ailing father's estate, now had competition from a stepmother of his own generation and a half-sister young enough to be Andrew's own daughter. Philip Kehoe's arthritis had crippled the old man terribly; he now used canes to lug his heavy body through the house. His dependence on Frances was all-consuming.[25]

Relations between the elder Kehoe and his son deteriorated. It took a terrible tragedy to change all that.

Sunday, September 17, 1911. Accounts differ as to how the incident began. One story has Frances and her daughter picking hickory nuts in the forest behind the Kehoe home, then coming home to make lunch.[26] A different version holds that Mrs. Kehoe was in town and hurried home to fix the noontime meal.[27] Regardless, Frances went into the kitchen, a small room in the back of the house. A large stove dominated the space. For the times it was a state-of-the art apparatus with a large fuel source on top. Again accounts differ as to the source of power: one story claims that the stove ran on gasoline;[28] another says it was oil.[29] Despite its enormous size, the stove had a small defect. Frances always had to light the pilot before she could use the appliance. The ignition temperature of a gas stove is generally about 495 degrees Fahrenheit; an ignited match head ranges between 600 and 800 degrees.

Frances struck a match and touched it to the pilot light. The world changed in an instant.

A flame of enormous size and power whooshed out of the stove, engulfing Frances in a mini-tornado of fire. A petroleum-based fire, such as gas or oil, generates incredible heat, somewhere in the range of 1,650 degrees at its lowest point to around 2,280 at its hottest. It takes 2,750 degrees to melt the iron of a stove. Human flesh is another matter.

Skin is the largest organ of the body. It covers the dermis, an underlayer that separates the outer portion from fat, muscle, and bone, vital organs, arteries and veins, and an intricate web of nerves. The human body is filled with water, which can take the form of blood, spinal fluid, or bone marrow. Fat is a sponge filled with water. Some parts of the body are more water rich than others, such as skin and muscles, which hold about 75 percent of the average person's bodily liquid. All told, the typical human body is 60 to 75 percent water.

Whether sitting in a pot or circulating inside a person, water boils at 212 degrees, transforming liquid into steam. When a human body is subject to these extreme temperatures, the intense heat burns through muscle and bone, organs and fat. The skin gives way, melting as though it were candle wax.

Frances was in agony. She stumbled through the kitchen, desperately trying to put out the fire consuming her body. Her screams rang throughout the house, unearthly sounds bouncing off the walls, careening down hallways, through open windows, out into the yard.

Irene flew in from outside toward the terrible sounds, fingers white-knuckle tight around the hickory nut bucket handle. Her mother was unrecognizable, a body flailing about, arms pounding at its flame-engulfed head.

Philip Kehoe moved as quickly as he could to the kitchen, canes dragging him inch by inch. He was helpless, drenched in the psychological agony of a man who is desperately needed yet trapped in a body that cannot respond.

Andrew heard the loud thunder of the stove, a split second of silence, then the piercing screams of his young stepmother. In a moment he was in the kitchen. Thinking fast, he grabbed a pitcher of water and flung it on the inferno that was Frances.

In gas stove fires, flour or baking powder is the quickest way to smother flame, effectively using a concentrated rain of particles to stop the blaze from spreading. Water, which does not mix with petroleum, is useless and in fact dangerous in these situations. In essence, water spreads gasoline or oil into a thin layer. In a fire this causes rapid spread of the flame.

The water Andrew used to douse the fire only made the situation worse. The flames raced across Frances's body, rapidly liquefying what little skin she had left.

Somehow the fire was quelled. Andrew and Irene took the moaning, smoking Frances to a bedroom where they tried to make her comfortable. Frances's skin was blackened, her muscles roasted to the bone. A hellish stench permeated the house.

All the while Philip Kehoe valiantly pushed on toward his wife.

Any movement sent massive pain surges throughout Frances's ruined body. Since the Kehoe home had no telephone, Andrew and his half sister headed for the Murphy house, their closest neighbor, to call a doctor.

Hettie Murphy was in her kitchen, preparing lunch for the family. She lived with her husband and in-laws, who were overjoyed that Hettie was pregnant.

Years later, when asked about her experience that day, Hettie remembered a simple knock at the door, a nonchalant rap, not the adrenaline-charged banging of someone in a dire situation.

She dusted off her hands, then politely went to answer the door. Hettie greeted Kehoe, who stood on the front porch, seemingly without a care in the world. He might well have come over asking to borrow a shovel.

Instead, Kehoe asked Hettie to call the local doctor. When she asked if someone was sick, Kehoe's answer was calm.

"No," he told Hettie. "Frannie got burned." It was as though she had spilled a pot of boiling water on her foot.

He also asked Hettie to call a priest.[30]

They gathered around Frances with Philip, a man lost in dire thought and bottomless grief. Frances, little more than a blackened lump of a woman, cried in tortured pain. There was nothing for the doctor to do but watch the priest deliver the last rites.

Outside, beneath the window, the family dog gave a plaintive wail for his mistress.[31]

It would take years for questions to be asked about the tragedy and for hints to surface of Andrew Kehoe's possible involvement. In the wake of the school bombing, the story of Frances Kehoe rustled throughout Bath. One version of the tale claimed the tragedy happened when Kehoe was just fourteen rather than forty—a natural mistake when stories are spread through rumor.[32]

Did Kehoe arrange his stepmother's horrific death? Having tinkered with gadgets and machinery since his childhood, he conceivably had the know-how to rig a stove for detonation.

There is—of course—no way to find the answer; it is another part of the labyrinthine mystery of Andrew P. Kehoe.

◆ ◆ ◆

Philip Kehoe had not expected to outlive his young wife. Now filled with pain in both body and soul, the elder Kehoe's condition deteriorated further.

Andrew had other things on his mind besides his stepmother's death and his father's declining health. Now in his early forties, he resumed an old courtship with Ellen Price—known to all by her nickname, "Nellie"—whom he'd met years before at Michigan State. The two briefly dated as students (such as dating was in the late nineteenth century), then parted before Kehoe left for Saint Louis. Now was as good a time as any to get reintroduced.

Nellie Price's background was similar to her beau's. Born in 1875, she was the daughter of an Irish Catholic immigrant, Patrick Price, and his wife Mary Ann. Her mother died when Nellie was just eighteen. As the eldest daughter in a family of five, Nellie was charged with raising the children. They lived in Bath, where Patrick Price farmed the land owned by his older brother Laurence. In 1908, Patrick Price moved to Lansing, where he and the children would be closer to his beloved brother Laurence.[33]

A Civil War veteran and successful Lansing businessman, Laurence Price made his fortune in the fledgling automobile industry, opening a factory to manufacture car parts for Henry Ford. Wealthy and with a passion for public service, Price turned to politics. He won a few elective offices, making him a well-known and important figure in many powerful Lansing circles.[34]

On May 14, 1912, just seven months after Frances Kehoe's gruesome end, Andrew and Nellie wed.[35] They moved to Tecumseh, where Kehoe resumed work on his father's farm. The old man, now confined to a wheelchair, died on January 8, 1915.[36]

The couple largely kept to themselves, though they briefly attended a nearby Catholic church. When the original parish church was torn down, congregants were assessed a fee to pay for a new sanctuary. Andrew and Nellie Kehoe's share came to four hundred dollars. As if in a nod to his father's feelings about taxation, Kehoe simply ignored the bill. One of the parish priests called at the Kehoe home to collect the money. In no uncertain terms, the clergyman was ordered off the property. Kehoe never returned to the congregation. It was said he also forbade his wife to worship at the new church.[37]

Another story was told of Kehoe's belief that a neighbor had cheated him in a livestock sale. After buying eight steers, Kehoe penned the animals in a clover field on his property. The field, wet from a recent rainstorm, proved deadly. Two of the cattle bloated badly from the damp feed and quickly died. Kehoe harvested their carcasses, sold the hides in town, then returned to the man from whom he bought the animals. He demanded half his payment back, an unreasonable request the seller naturally would not honor. The argument that ensued between the two is lost through the mist of decades. Yet people noticed that for some time whenever they crossed each other's path in town, Kehoe remained silent, turning whatever thoughts he had inward.[38]

◆ ◆ ◆

In 1916, Nellie's uncle was nominated as a Democratic candidate for the U.S. Senate. Although Laurence Price lost to Michigan's Republican incumbent Charles E. Townsend, he was still a formidable presence throughout the Lansing area.[39] When Price died on February 12, 1917, he left behind a considerable estate with money going to a variety of charities and relatives. His house and land in Bath—Nellie's childhood home—remained in the family.

The eighty-acre farm was ideal for Kehoe and his wife. At the center of the property was a three-story home with a roomy front porch and an elegant set of bay windows on the second floor. More windows filled the exterior, providing plenty of portals for sunshine. The good-sized spread had a roomy barn and separate chicken coop. Its land was rich, perfect for a good variety of crops. To the east was a wooded area, lush and green in the spring and summer and a kaleidoscope of colors come autumn. It was a showcase for the region, a well-kept estate that seemed like a regal memorial to the late Laurence Price.

Kehoe approached Richard Price, another of Laurence's brothers, to see if he could buy the property. Richard, along with Laurence's widow Beulah and their attorney Joseph H. Dunnebacke, served as executors of the departed's business interests. A deal was negotiated. Kehoe would buy the property for twelve thousand dollars. He would make a six-thousand-dollar down payment with the balance and interest held in a mortgage to the Laurence Price estate. On March 27, 1919, the deed was turned over to Andrew Kehoe.[40] Once he sold his place in Tecumseh, Kehoe and Nellie could move to her childhood home in Bath.

Kehoe placed his farm in the hands of a real estate agent. Two weeks later an interested buyer stopped by to speak with Kehoe. Ironically, it was the same man who had entered into the ill-fated agreement with Kehoe over the cattle. The two, it seemed, had managed to work past their old rift into a tentative truce. When the man asked if the property was on the market, Kehoe exploded. "Yes," he snapped back, "but why in the hell didn't you come two weeks ago, before I turned it over to the real estate hands and I would have saved the commission!"[41]

Regardless of this new spat, Kehoe sold the farm to his adversary for eight thousand dollars. The down payment was made on the Bath property. Kehoe and Nellie packed up their belongings and readied themselves for a new home.

Before leaving, Kehoe made one last business transaction. There were fifteen cords of wood on his Tecumseh farm. Obviously this wouldn't be packed up for the move. Kehoe approached a neighbor, offering to sell the entire load at half the regular price. At a dollar fifty per cord this was a considerable bargain, yet Kehoe's neighbor amiably turned it down. Like every farmer in the region, he had all the wood he needed and then some.

Kehoe insisted the man go for this bargain. Again he was refused, and once more Kehoe pushed the sale.

Kehoe made it clear that he did not want to leave the wood for the new owner. The house and farm were sold, but the fifteen cords of wood were still Kehoe's and he'd be damned before leaving something on his former property that hadn't been bought and paid for. Ultimately the neighbor acquiesced to Kehoe's pressure.[42]

Andrew Kehoe was nothing if not dogged.

Chapter 3

~~~~~~

DAWN OF A DECADE

~~~~~~

The 1920s really started on January 16, 1919, when the U.S. Congress ratified the Eighteenth Amendment to the Constitution. Section 1 of the new law read "After one year from the ratification of this article the manufacture, sale, or transportation of liquors within, the importation thereof into, or the exportation thereof from the United States and all territory subject to the jurisdiction thereof for beverage purposes is hereby prohibited." The amendment was followed on October 28 by the Volstead Act, a regulation named after its chief sponsor, the clout-heavy Minnesota congressman Andrew Volstead. This new law banned the sale of adult beverages, defining booze as better than 0.5 percent alcohol used for "intoxicating purposes." Both edicts were filed together under the dirty name "Prohibition."

Naturally, outlawing a high-demand product is about as easy to enforce as repealing the law of gravity. The liquor industry easily found new routes to a thirsty public. Gangsters in New York, Chicago, and other major cities developed a thriving—if sometimes violent and deadly—underground business. Morals codified by law were gleefully ignored. It was a new era dubbed the Jazz Age by its poster child, scribe F. Scott Fitzgerald, author of the quintessential 1920s novel *The Great Gatsby*. In big cities throughout the country bathtub gin flowed, hemlines rose a few notches as flappers danced the Charleston, the sounds of jazz blew from bandstands in smoky clubs, and old-fashioned morals were stomped into ashes by the fun.

Some of the seedier elements of the day took hold near the Bath area. Al Capone, that most notorious of all gangsters, often headed to nearby Lansing to visit a "friend," a low-level and anonymous gang member who had resettled in Michigan after a Windy City killing went horribly wrong. This former thug reinvented himself as an honest businessman, opening a profitable fruit and vegetable market. Local restaurants relied on the store for their produce. Still, business was business, and the owner kept vestigial ties to his former employer, letting Capone occasionally use the legitimate fruit and vegetable establishment as a warehouse for contraband booze shipped in from Canada.[1]

Capone had a more pressing reason to visit his former associate after the murder of Chicago prosecutor William McSwiggin. The crusading attorney, son of a Chicago cop, had led a double life. A good guy by day, McSwiggin enjoyed slumming with Al Capone and his crew during off hours.

One night McSwiggin made the mistake of getting into a car owned by two of Big Al's bootlegging rivals, the O'Donnell brothers, Myles and William (aka "Klondike"). When the O'Donnells' automobile was seen driving through the streets of Capone's territory, loyal members of the gang (and possibly Scarface himself) followed. When the time was right, Big Al's men opened fire. Tommy guns spat angry bursts at the O'Donnells, filling the night air with the stink of metal, gunpowder, and blood.

The offending siblings escaped serious harm, but the unlucky prospector was hit in the back and neck by a hail of bullets. The O'Donnells picked up McSwiggin's lifeless body, removed all identification, and dumped the hapless corpse in a deserted woods.

Once the body was found and finally identified, newspapers and politicians unleashed enough righteous indignation to fill the Chicago River and then some. McSwiggin was a very public official with a very public father, and there were very public demands that something be done. The sweep came down hard. Several of Capone's joints were raided; so was his South Side home. But when McSwiggin was laid to rest Capone still remained at large. (Ironically, McSwiggin's final resting place, Mount Carmel Cemetery in the western suburbs of Chicago, was also the last stop for some of Chicago's most notorious gangsters, including Capone himself.)[2]

Meanwhile, Capone secretly fled to Michigan to hide out with old *paisan* cum fruit peddler. In an unexpected turn of events, Scarface fell in love with the area. He spent several summers in Lansing where he openly (if not brazenly) walked about town. Eventually he bought a cottage on a glorified pond dubbed "Round Lake," a small resort area about five miles from Bath. Not one to take anything for granted, Capone also brought his top triggermen and bodyguards, "Machine Gun" Jack McGurn and Frank "The Enforcer" Nitti whenever he hung out at Round Lake in case their services were required.[3]

Capone's presence amounted to little more than a rumor in the area since *nobody* discussed Scarface openly. One family living about eight miles from the Capone property thought he was nothing more than a "pretty nice neighbor."[4]

Other than the "pretty nice neighbor," Bath generally steered clear of the notorious bootlegging economy. One old-timer claimed he occasionally heard someone noisily clanking bottles late at night;[5] another 1920s Bath resident retorted that this was just so much nonsense.[6] The truth is probably somewhere between the two stories.

People looking for a night out headed to some of the dance halls outside of town (including one near Capone's Round Lake hideaway), though most Bath residents preferred Loving's Dance Hall for a carefree night of jazz and dancing. The establishment had a generator to light the dance floor. The combination of music, dancing, and electricity was a powerful weekend draw to Bath's otherwise straitlaced townsfolk.[7]

But rural bootleggers and electrified dance halls aside, Bath was largely immune to the spirit of the day, a true bastion from the loose behavior that was swallowing Detroit to the east and Chicago to the west. The Roaring Twenties roared well outside of Bath. The little hamlet was a throwback to a more idyllic portrait of small-town America where everyone knew their neighbors and doors were left unlocked at night. Bath's growth in the early twentieth century was practically a boom by 1920. Proximity to the Michigan Central Railroad made the town a good way station between Lansing and all points beyond. Farmers shipped produce via the freight services with six trains passing through town every day. About three hundred people called themselves residents, utilizing the bank, local dry goods stores, a pharmacy, and not one, but two garages for automobile repair.

Several folks in town owned Ford cars or trucks. Locals referred to their automotive vehicles with the handy catchall word *machine,* as in

"There goes Albert Detluff in his machine!" Detluff, a blacksmith by trade, kept up with the times, dividing his business between auto repair and shoeing horses. Despite the growth of the automobile culture, Bath's equine culture wasn't completely outmoded.

For more sedate entertainment and gatherings, people relied on the Community Hall. Offering an alternative to the sinful delights of the roadhouses, the hall was a place for dances and get-togethers where young and old could meet in a socially respectable clime. The three-story structure housed meeting rooms and a ballroom outfitted with a stage, the perfect spot for small-town events. Local chapters of the international fraternal organization the Odd Fellows, along with their women's auxiliary the Rebekahs, also met in the Community Hall.[8]

From September through June Bath's Friday Afternoon Club met twice a month at the Community Hall for socializing and games. The group, as the lyrics of the official club song emphasized, stood for purity, sharing, and the "aim to do our best."[9]

What Bath still needed was electricity on demand. A gas-powered generator was necessary for electric power—and even then the contraptions couldn't provide twenty-four-hour, nonstop power unless the owner kept a close eye on the fuel tanks. A few homeowners, farmers, and businessmen did use generators. But the lack of instant power didn't impede village life. Indeed, Bath was a thriving model of self-efficiency in the wake of the Great War.

For those looking for electrically powered entertainment beyond dancing, there was always a moving picture show in Lansing. Douglas Fairbanks ruled the silver screen for drama and adventure, while his real-life spouse Mary Pickford provided a sense of innocent romance. For a good laugh Charlie Chaplin was all the rage. Then there were the slapstick movies of Mack Sennett and his stable of comedians. A staple of the Sennett films was dynamite. Watching the flickering images, one learned that dynamite could be smuggled into cigars or birthday candles to blow up mustachioed villains or hapless heroes. Dynamite certainly was the bane of Sennett's crazed Keystone Kops. The powerful explosive, as portrayed in these comedies, would blacken a victim's face, send his hair into crazy configurations, and throw him into a daze.

What dynamite couldn't do, according to the movies, was really harm anyone.

Chapter 4

·····························

NEW MAN IN TOWN

·····························

They seemed like good neighbors.

A few old-timers remembered Nellie when she was a little girl living on her uncle's property, and later as a loving surrogate mom to her siblings after their mother died. Although years had passed, Nellie was a welcome face in familiar climes.

Her husband was, to say the least, an interesting character who had a touch of class about him coupled with more than a few eccentricities. The man could be a real dichotomy at times.

While Nellie stayed in Lansing with her sisters, Kehoe moved their belongings to the three-story house. A rented truck brought furniture, shipped via the Michigan Central Railroad, from the depot downtown. Kehoe had three horses and what one person remembered as "some very fine thoroughbred hogs."[1] More impressive was his two loads of farm equipment. Unlike many farmers in the region, Kehoe's machinery was modern and well beyond the means of the average person in Bath. Clearly Nellie had married a man of some measure.

David Harte, whose farm lay across the road from Kehoe's, helped his new neighbor unload his furniture and move it into the house. Although

Kehoe tried to contact Nellie by telephone, he could not get in touch with his wife. Where was Mrs. Kehoe, asked Harte. Kehoe wouldn't give a direct answer. She was, he implied, at church.[2]

Harte gave it no thought. It seemed a reasonable enough answer.

Despite the modern farm equipment, which Kehoe clearly relished, the couple lacked automotive transportation of their own. Other than his tractor, Kehoe owned no machine, neither truck nor car. When it was time to shop for groceries or farm supplies, the Kehoes relied on the kindness of their neighbors. Lulu Harte regularly drove Nellie Kehoe into Lansing for shopping.[3]

As the new man in town Kehoe exhibited a polite, friendly demeanor. In fact, he always was ready and willing to lend his hand to any proceedings. When later asked if Kehoe had ever caused trouble or problems, one man replied, "not a particle."[4]

Job Sleight, like many farmers in the region, still worked his land using old-fashioned methods: the ox and the plow. He was fascinated by his new neighbor's gas-powered tractor.

At times Sleight stood alongside of the road watching Kehoe work. Eventually he introduced himself, explaining his interest in modern techniques. Kehoe extended his hand to Sleight, exchanged a few jovial words, then invited his neighbor to try the tractor himself.[5]

Beyond his modern equipment, Kehoe clearly was not a standard issue farmer. Almost immediately he set himself apart from his neighbors in both person and practice.

Farming is dirty work. It requires digging deep into the soil and getting dirt under fingernails and into ears, streaking the face, sticking to clothing, and clodding deep into the soles of work boots. Equipment maintenance adds to the mess. Gasoline and grease combine for a smell unlike anything else, a cluster of aromas tangy with oily fumes. Petroleum has a way of permeating skin, hair, and clothing. A good farmer literally wears his work proudly.

Coveralls, a standard for any farmer, were not in Kehoe's wardrobe. He approached his work like a businessman suiting up for the office. He always wore clean suits, a vest, and shiny shoes. There was never a hair out of place as he worked the land, riding his tractor like an emperor parading through his domain. It was a marvel to watch this clean-cut, well-dressed man plowing and planting under the hot sun, rarely breaking a sweat. Should he stain his shirt with perspiration or soil, Kehoe went inside the house for a replacement. Tools were always stacked neatly in his shed, never a hoe or rake out of place. Anyone who visited the farm marveled that the Kehoe farm was a model of order and his barn was cleaner than many houses in Bath.[6]

His land was neat as well. Stumps and boulders inevitably pockmark farm fields like raisins in a cinnamon roll, sticking out halfway in odd places or buried haphazardly just beneath the surface. As he had demonstrated in Tecumseh, Kehoe was a master at removing the protrusions using dynamite and pyrotol. Explosions were often heard on the property, although the sound was certainly not out of place on any farmer's land. Dynamite and pyrotol were efficient and fast, albeit loud and a little dangerous. Easy to get and easy to store, these two powerful agents were as natural as a plow in breaking up the land.

Farmers understood that real explosives weren't something out of a Mack Sennett comedy: dynamite and pyrotol could cause severe damage, sending debris high into the air and possibly killing operators or bystanders. It took experienced hands to set up and detonate the potentially deadly substances.

In no time at all, other farmers in Bath considered Kehoe their go-to man in the proper care and use of dynamite.

In a town largely populated by families with children, the Kehoes were something of an oddity. Most residents could trace their lineages back a couple of generations to the town's founders and first residents. Cushman, Barnard, Peacock, Hart, and Harte (two branches of the same family) were names as deeply important to Bath as its farm-based economy. Not that the town was hostile to strangers. The Perrones, an Italian immigrant family, was a much-loved presence throughout Bath.[7]

The Kehoes were different in that they were older and childless. Sure, there were townsfolk the same age as the couple, but they were—for the most part—either parents or grandparents. Not that anyone would ever hold this against Andrew and Nellie. Everyone liked them; they were good people. Lulu Harte, in the course of their shopping trips to Lansing, developed an amiable though not terribly close friendship with Nellie.

The Kehoes were active in social events in town as well, becoming stalwart members of the Friday Afternoon Club. They particularly enjoyed playing euchre, a regionally popular card game. Euchre pitted four people in two partnerships. Kehoe was particularly adept at the complicated game, although he often annoyed opponents by pointing out par-

Fig. 2. Andrew and Nellie Kehoe. *(Courtesy of the Bath School Museum.)*

ticularly bungling errors or violations of the rules. The couple was also good at puzzles, and Kehoe created complicated metal devices that others had to untangle. Some club members noticed that other than his outbursts during euchre, Kehoe seemed to think over every word before speaking and never talked much of his personal life.[8]

Kehoe became a regular fixture at local farm bureaus, organizations where farmers met to discuss techniques, economics, and other issues related to their lives and work. He fast became a respected individual known for his quick mind, expertise in modern technology, and growing interest in local affairs, someone who eagerly volunteered his time and was a stalwart voice at bureaus and granges throughout the region. It seemed the influence of Philip Kehoe was finally manifesting itself in his son.[9]

By all appearances, Nellie had done well. Her husband was a good man with a few personality quirks but otherwise had a great passion for life and helping others.

Yet there were moments that revealed a darker edge to Andrew Kehoe. David Harte discovered this early on. The Hartes, like many farm families, let their dogs have the run of their land. One of the family pets, a terrier, enjoyed scampering in the front yard where the Harte home faced the Kehoe residence. After a hard day of yipping and yapping, the dog usually came home. But in March of 1920, nearly a year after the Kehoes moved to Bath, the terrier went missing.

Various stories were told about what happened to the dog. According to one account, Kehoe claimed he shot the dog accidentally.[10] Another had Lulu asking Kehoe if he had seen the dog. Yes, he told her, the terrier was burying a bone along the fence on Kehoe's property and he shot the damned nuisance.[11] A third story had Lulu coming back from a trip to Lansing with Nellie. The dog was poisoned, and Lulu knew in her heart that Kehoe had killed it.[12]

Regardless of how it died, it is a given that Kehoe killed the dog. There was no dustup over the incident. Kehoe and Harte still spoke as neighbors and farmers, often helping one another thresh their crops.

Lulu Harte, however, no longer offered Nellie Kehoe rides to Lansing.[13]

Chapter 5

THE BATH CONSOLIDATED SCHOOL

In general terms, farming was man's work; boys consequently learned from their fathers how to work the land. Girls, as expected, were taught the basics of keeping house from their mothers and grandmothers.

But standard subjects—reading, writing, arithmetic—were better served by an organized system, no matter how rudimentary or sparse that education might be. In 1840 Bath's first schoolhouse, a one-room log cabin, was built by Peter Finch, whose wife was trained as a teacher. Records indicate that between seven to ten children—the majority of them girls—attended. Though confined to one room, the school was a cozy building complete with a good-sized fireplace to keep students warm during the winter months.[1]

The facility was a successful venture until the arrival of a traveling minister come to spread the Gospel in the wilderness. As a welcoming gesture, some of the schoolboys lit the fireplace. The blaze was warm, comforting, and too big. Flames jumped from the fireplace to the walls and ceiling, burning the schoolhouse to the ground.[2]

Perhaps this was a dream come true for the children, but parents didn't let education stop. Another log schoolhouse was built, and learning resumed.

A system of small schools ensued over the years. Often these spaces doubled as houses of worship for various denominations. The schools were usually identified by numbers, although a few acquired nicknames such as the Rose School (also known as Old Red) and the Peacock School. Buildings ranged from log cabins to more elaborate wooden frame buildings. Teachers, as was the custom of the day, were hired on a year-to-year basis. In 1856, one woman hired to teach six days a week made thirty-three cents a day for her work. Some schools were funded by government grants, with construction a community effort.[3]

Typically most children completed school at the tenth-grade level. At their peak in the early twentieth century, ten small schoolhouses—some one-room and others multi-grade facilities—served Bath and the surrounding region.[4]

As the community grew, so did the need for a more organized and centrally located facility. A new idea was floated: consolidate all the small schools in one large building and extend educational opportunity through the twelfth grade.

Such change does not come without opposition, and this radical move had its detractors. The idea of consolidation raised numerous challenges that many people felt were insurmountable. How could nearly three hundred children be transported from home to school? Who would feed them lunch? Where would the teachers come from? What body would oversee the new school?

And most important—in some eyes—who was going to pay for all this?

A meeting was held on July 22, 1921. A high-ranking state official was brought in to make the case for consolidation. An official vote was held three days later. The referendum passed. Now came the hard work.[5]

By mid-August a school board was up and running and the hunt for a central location was under way. A hill near downtown Bath provided an ideal spot. The new school would be a shining landmark overlooking the town, symbolically representing a higher ideal and bright future.[6]

"A consolidated school is expensive in a small community," wrote Monty Ellsworth, a local resident, a few years later in his chronicle of the Kehoe bombing. "But there are a great many other things to look at. The children don't have to wade through the snow and mud, they are picked up at the door. A great many people appreciate not having their children playing along the road with rough children and standing a chance of being attacked by some lawless ruffian. The parents can feel that their children are safe from the time they leave the door to the time they are brought back, the bus drivers being selected from the most responsible men of the community who make application. . . . The consolidated school is a help in a great many ways; the children have the same class-mates up to the time they graduate. In the rural schools they work along until they pass the eighth grade and then go into a strange school. In some cases they are large for their age and this causes them a handicap. . . . Teacher have to be farther advanced to teach in a consolidated school than they do in a common country school. . . . [W]hen everything is taken into consideration, the consolidated school is the cheapest and best way of education."[7]

A former school building in Bath that had housed grades one through ten was salvageable and could be moved to the new location. This, it was decided, could form the basis of the new building. Class-rooms for the elementary grades would meet on the first floor with high school students taking the second story.[8]

On November 12, 1921, a vote was held on a bond proposal to fund the new school. Out of seventy-six votes, only twenty people opposed the plan. With the new school came a bond for $43,000.[9] Eight thousand dollars already raised by the school board would pay for the athletic fields and lighting plants; the additional $35,000 would come from property taxes at the rate of $12.26 per $1,000 of property valuation.[10]

Architects and builders were engaged. Work began. Gradually a building rose. Anticipation grew.

Next was the human element.

Emory E. Huyck was born on July 3, 1894, on a small farm outside But-ternut, Michigan, one of the eleven children of Mr. and Mrs. William Huyck. After completing high school, Huyck attended the Ferris Insti-tute, a small college in Big Rapids, Michigan. Like so many young men of his generation, he volunteered for military service when the United States entered the Great War. He served as a training officer at Camp Custer in Augusta, Michigan, teaching English-language skills to raw-boned recruits.[11] After his discharge from the army, Huyck returned to school for his bachelor's degree. He majored in agricultural studies at Michigan State College and while still a student married Ethel Huyck, a schoolteacher by profession.[12]

Between his agricultural degree and his work as a military educator, Huyck was considered ideal for his new job of superintendent of the

Fig. 3. The newly built Bath Consolidated School. *(Courtesy of the Bath School Museum.)*

Bath Consolidated School. He was young, talented, and showed great potential. He could do double duty as an administrator and teacher. Best of all, since he was barely out of school himself Huyck's initial salary could be set relatively low for a man in his position.[13]

Teachers were hired. Arrangements were made for their housing with separate facilities for women and men.[14]

Transportation was another issue. In the one-room schoolhouse era, students simply walked to school. A consolidated facility required more sophisticated means of travel. Six motor-driven vehicles were initially acquired, five of which were standard buses. The sixth was a Model T Ford fitted with a detachable body. In fall, winter, and spring, children were transported to and from school in this machine; in summer the body was removed and the Model T used for farm work.[15] A seventh bus was a horse-drawn wagon equipped with a potbellied stove so passengers could stay warm during cold Michigan winters.[16]

When the school opened in fall 1922 with 236 students, it ushered in a new era for the community.[17] Modern education had come to Bath. The 1920s promised to be a time of beneficent growth.

◆ ◆ ◆

Perhaps Mark Twain put it best when he wrote in *Pudd'nhead Wilson's New Calendar,* "In the first place God made idiots. This was for practice. Then He made School Boards."

The new trustees wanted things plain and simple: administration of the school was their responsibility; oversight of teaching went to Huyck. On the surface it seemed like a good idea. The majority of school board members had previous experience running the one-room schoolhouse districts. But the consolidated school offered different challenges.

With a small regional school board, it was inevitable that many members would be friends or relatives of people living in the district. Conflicts of interest, such as giving bus contracts to relatives or hiring friends of friends, were usually overlooked. The school board also preferred to hold its meetings in private rather than opening the proceedings to the public.[18] Most important, keeping a good school in line with modern educational standards required a constant flow of money. The funding came, of course, from local taxes.

In one respect, the money certainly was well spent. Huyck pushed hard to earn the school that holy grail of education: accreditation. Accreditation would prove that the Bath Consolidated School was serious about the future of its students. Essentially educational accreditation is a quality certification granted by a third party, an assurance that the school has set rigorous goals to achieve excellence. In the case of the Bath Consolidated School, the accrediting agency was the University of Michigan. The criteria were basic: specific educational backgrounds were required for all teachers, classes must meet Michigan state regulations, and members of the faculty and administration must adhere to proper standards of conduct for people of their profession. Huyck proved himself worthy of the task, and accreditation was granted in May 1925, not quite three years after the school opened. With accreditation came financial resources in the form of federal and state Home Economic Aid and other government grants.[19]

In the wake of the Great War, a recession stalked the global economy. The United States also experienced a downturn, though not to the extent suffered by its European counterparts.

This was of little comfort to farmers struggling to make ends meet, particularly with increased property assessments to pay for the consolidated school. Discontent percolated in several quarters, leading to considerable discussion about how the Bath School Board was handling its financial concerns. In this respect, Kehoe most assuredly was his father's son. Like Philip Kehoe before him, Andrew was vocal in his discontent over tax oversight. And he was ready to back up his words with action.[20]

The school board treasurer, Enos Peacock, came up for reelection. The Peacock name was well known throughout the community: Enos's forebears had built the one-room Peacock School. Although Peacock had always been considered an excellent steward of the people's money, Kehoe led a coalition demanding new leadership rather than the "old boy's network" that seemed to permeate the board.

The election was held on July 14. Six men, including Kehoe and Peacock, were running for the trustee position. A winner would be decided when one man received a majority of all votes cast; with six candidates on the ballot, this was no easy task. Yet Kehoe was the top vote getter on the first poll. He held on to the lead through each vote, finally winning a board position on the sixth canvass.

His was a three-year position due to expire in July 1927.[21]

Kehoe was sworn in a week later as one of two new board members. Perhaps in a nod to his fiscal prudence, Kehoe's fellow trustees elected him treasurer. School board meetings were inevitably long, as members wrestled over standard educational and administrative issues. But Kehoe's presence brought a new element to the proceedings.

Superintendent Hyuck always attended board meetings; most board members felt it was good protocol for a responsible school administrator.

Kehoe saw Huyck's presence in a different light. To him, it seemed like a control factor. The administrator/teacher should do his job and let the board handle the rest. Kehoe was elected to serve the people's interests and was determined to fulfill that responsibility. He demanded that Huyck be banned from board meetings. This flew in the face of other trustees' preferences to say nothing of Michigan law. Kehoe was told that in order to receive state funding the superintendent's presence was required during the official assemblies of any board of education.[22] Despite the superintendent's popularity in the community, both professionally and socially, Huyck remained the subject of Kehoe's scorn.

Kehoe and Huyck openly loathed one another. It was a strange relationship, one that escalated over time. It was as though Kehoe had tagged Huyck as someone beyond a mere adversary. No, Huyck was a person who had to learn his place and role in the community, and Kehoe was the man who knew just how to make that happen. Huyck, on the other hand, wanted what was best for his students and would do what he had to to ensure their academic success.

Their animosity increased when it came to Huyck's salary. In what must have been a personal victory to Kehoe, the superintendent's vacation was cut to one week a year and his annual pay increase reduced to one hundred dollars instead of the customary two hundred. Next Kehoe challenged the patronage system of school business. Bus service was routinely contracted to Ward Kyes, who happened to be son of board member Melville Kyes. It didn't matter that Ward's bids were higher than other potential contractors: Ward was Mel's son, and that's how business was done. Kehoe fought like hell to stop the practice, but his challenge was easily defeated. Some things just weren't tinkered with.[23]

Despite his cantankerous approach to board politics (when things didn't go his way, he often motioned for meetings to be adjourned),[24] Kehoe's sense of fiscal responsibility did earn him begrudging respect in some quarters and praise in others. As treasurer his books were always— *always*—balanced to the penny. This reputation for meticulous accounting came into play when Maude Detluff, the township clerk and wife of the blacksmith/auto repairman (and fellow school board member) Albert Detluff, unexpectedly passed away in April 1925. Local Republican Party officials asked Kehoe if he would be interested in completing the last year of Maude Detluff's term, a part-time position with some remuneration. A stepping-stone to something bigger, it seemed. With his place on the school board and now as township clerk, Kehoe had the potential to make a personal impact on the community. He took the offer.[25]

His power didn't last long. A year later, in the next general election, party officials picked another candidate for township clerk. Despite his talent for balancing ledgers, Kehoe's confrontational reputation on the school board ultimately did him in.[26] Although it was obvious his presence was no longer required, Kehoe and his wife sat quietly throughout the nominating process for clerk held at the Community Hall. He said not a word throughout the proceedings, giving no indication of how he felt.

He would make one last try at public office. Three years later, in spring 1927, Kehoe would be nominated for the position of county justice of the peace. Again he would be soundly defeated; again he and Nellie would be present at the town meeting where the voting was held, and once more they would make no fuss after the loss.[27]

In these defeats, it seemed, Kehoe simply turned his emotions and thoughts inward.[28]

◆　◆　◆

On July 3, 1776, as his dream of an independent government free from British rule was finally coming to fruition, John Adams wrote to his wife Abigail with some thoughts on how future generations should celebrate America's birth. Independence Day, Adams said, must be "solemnized with Pomp and Parade, with Shews, Games, Sports, Guns, Bells, Bonfires and Illuminations from one End of this Continent to the other from this Time forward forever more."[29]

On July 4, 1924, blasts echoed throughout the farmlands surrounding the Kehoe place. These were no ordinary stump-blasting explosions; any passing fool might have though the Great War was being reenacted on Kehoe's property.

The ruckus put a scare into Sydney and Charlotte Howell. When they asked Nellie Kehoe about her husband's unconventional fireworks, she jokingly calmed their fears.

"The little boy is having some fun," she said.[30]

◆　◆　◆

David Harte needed to borrow a seat for his old wagon and figured he'd get one from his neighbor. He went across the road to where Kehoe was working his fields, driving his horses into a froth as they dragged a manure spreader. The animals pulled mightily but not hard enough for their master. Onward, onward, Kehoe pushed them, past their breaking point. Sometime that night, one of the horses gave up the ghost.

The next day a truck from the local rendering works picked up the remains. When Harte came by to fetch the wagon seat, he mentioned it to Kehoe. "I see you had bad luck with your horse," he said.

"Yes, damn him," Kehoe snapped back. "He ought to have been killed years ago. He didn't pull and we had a mixup and when I got through with him he was dead."[31]

First the Harte dog, now his own horse. It seemed Kehoe had a nasty disposition with animals.

◆　◆　◆

A school requires consistent and broad-thinking changes. Huyck wanted investments for the educational future; Kehoe saw mounting expenses at the burden of the taxpayer. Every meeting Huyck had with the accreditation body meant more spending. Decisions on what was needed were made hand-in-hand between the University of Michigan's accreditation representatives and Huyck, with the findings then presented to the board. Although his fellow trustees believed this was efficient, Kehoe only saw an out of control superintendent fighting for complete command of public spending.

Kehoe didn't understand why the accreditation committee wouldn't meet with the board; after all, who was paying for all these items? Huyck, he believed, was using taxpayer money as though it were a blank check.[32]

In the fall of 1926, Huyck's salary was raised another hundred dollars despite Kehoe's objections. Purchase items grew, and expenses rose. The students needed new books. Encyclopedia sets were required for the library. The girls' home economics classes and the boys' shop classes must have updated resources. Classrooms simply had to have pictures on the wall to enhance learning. At one point a fireproof safe made it to the purchase list. Another must-need item was basic playground equipment.[33]

Kehoe smoldered. Huyck remained cool. They were opponents tied together by the Bath Consolidated School. Whenever Kehoe and Huyck were in the same room, a certain tension existed. It crackled like static electricity.

Despite Kehoe's objections, Ward Kyes continued as one of Bath Consolidated's bus drivers. Every morning Ward picked up the children on his route and brought them home in the afternoon. Riding with Ward Kyes was as much a part of school as enrolling first graders in Miss Sterling's class; it was how things were done at Bath Consolidated.

Ward knew Kehoe didn't like him driving the bus, but he never held it against the man. In fact, he thought the cantankerous trustee was awfully smart. Whenever Ward attended school board meetings (and he did so to drive his father—board member Mel Kyes, who was blind in one eye—to school and back), he knew he could count on one thing: the ongoing agitation between Kehoe and Huyck. The bad blood between the two was like the joke about the elephant in the room: everyone knew it was there, but no one liked to talk about it.

Another thing Ward observed was that whenever a proposition was put before the board Kehoe inevitably would raise some kind of objection.

Ward's bus route never took him past the front of Kehoe's place unless the weather was bad; generally speaking, he always took a shortcut on the gravel road behind the property. Every afternoon Ward passed Kehoe's fence at about the same time.

And—Ward eventually noticed—Kehoe would be there, keeping his eye out for the bus. As Ward passed, Kehoe would look at his watch. It was almost like a ritual.

Nothing was ever said between the two about this routine. Ward figured Kehoe was just making sure the bus was running on time.[34]

Ruth Babcock, the home economics teacher, inadvertently provided Kehoe with an opportunity to take Huyck down a notch. The superintendent, a no-nonsense man, had difficulties with the headstrong teacher. Her educational methods didn't mesh with Huyck's ideas. There were confrontations between the two, battles for control over classroom decorum. At the end of the school year in 1926, Huyck recommended that Babcock's contract not be renewed. Babcock wrote down her observations and feelings about the superintendent, then provided these missives to the board of education. Kehoe demanded that the issue of Babcock's employment be reconsidered at the next meeting. The board agreed under the condition that Kehoe "investigate" the situation.

At the June meeting, Kehoe presented Babcock to the board. She explained in detail what was necessary for home economics—a vital part of any young woman's education—to succeed at the Bath Consolidated School. Babcock concluded her presentation by presenting the board with a table made by her students.

Kehoe's case for Babcock was reconsidered. A vote was taken. Huyck's decision stood.[35]

◆ ◆ ◆

In July of 1926, all of Bath turned out for the annual school meeting. It was asked that the voting rules be suspended so two pro-Huyck trustees could be reelected by acclamation. Through a series of procedural confusions the standard rules were followed, but Huyck's supporters were easily retained. Kehoe's tightfisted ways were clearly no longer in favor with the citizenry.

For the time being, Huyck retained a very public power over the obstinate trustee.[36]

◆ ◆ ◆

Kehoe's public life was spiraling. He was looking less like a crusader and more like a crank. Still, the buttoned-down farmer had some standing in the community as an active participant in school interests. As an expert electrician and mechanic, it was inevitable that his assistance would be sought—and it was freely volunteered—when various problems cropped at Bath Consolidated. One of Kehoe's more stellar contributions was his conquest over a bee infestation. Over the winter of 1925–26, a nest of bees hibernated beneath the school. As the furnace warmed up the school during those cold days, it inadvertently aroused the sleeping bees. They swept throughout halls and classrooms, stinging children and adults without mercy. The school board authorized Huyck and his principal, Floyd Huggett, to do something, *anything*, to stop these swarms. Twice they tried, and twice they failed. When a third infestation hit the school, Kehoe volunteered his services.

The bees were quickly annihilated. Just how Kehoe exterminated the pests is unclear. No one seemed to know what he did beneath the school, yet his solution did the trick.[37] (Years later, when athletic teams representing the Bath schools were named the Bees, rumors lingered that this was a throwback to the great bee infestation of 1925–26. In truth the moniker came from a contest in which a student submitted the name "Bees" in dubious honor of a swarm that had infested his father's workplace.)[38]

After demonstrating his ability with bees, Kehoe was asked if he wouldn't mind doing some much needed work on the school's electrical system. The board also authorized him to oversee other aspects of school's maintenance program. Plumbing. Tiling. General repairs. He agreed, did the chores without assistance, and was given unlimited access to the building, day or night, as needed.[39]

These jobs demanded intimate knowledge of the Bath Consolidated School building, inside and out, above and below. Kehoe learned about every corner, every crevice, every unused space. It was powerful knowledge for someone entrusted with upkeep and maintenance. The added duties certainly provided a unique perspective on the school for a trustee with his eyes on the future.

Job Sleight had a good reputation for helping neighbors who didn't own automobiles. All people had to do was ask when Sleight was headed to Lansing and he'd be happy to drive them where they needed to go, load their purchases into his truck, and drive them back to Bath. In October of 1925, Kehoe asked Sleight for a favor. Kehoe needed supplies for repairs at the school. His laundry list included bolts, pipes and fittings, and range boilers for the furnace. Sleight was happy to oblige. After the trip, he even helped unload the supplies at the school so Kehoe could begin his work.

Sleight always marveled at Kehoe's ingenuity. The man was a natural mechanic.[40]

On another occasion that fall, Kehoe telephoned Sleight for a ride. "Would you like to do me a favor and go to Jackson?" he asked. This was no small request; the round trip between the two towns was nearly a hundred miles.

"I presume I can," Sleight told Kehoe. "Maybe I can go soon. I have to go to town anyway." Sleight said he'd think it over and get back to Kehoe. As it turned out, Sleight made the trip the next day, though Kehoe couldn't go along. First, he explained, he needed to contact suppliers in order to make his purchases.

"What do you need?" asked Sleight.

"Pyrotol" was the reply. Kehoe explained that he wanted to blast some old tree stumps on the west side of his farm.

Going to Jackson just to pick up some pyrotol was an odd request, Sleight later thought. After all, Kehoe did a lot of volunteer work with local farm bureaus, and these organizations sold army surplus pyrotol to anyone who needed explosives.

Still, Sleight did the neighborly thing. Some time later the two men drove to an outfit just northeast of Jackson. They loaded ten boxes of pyrotol into Sleight's truck, a total of five hundred pounds. Kehoe also bought four boxes of blasting caps with which to set off the explosives.

"You don't want those caps anyplace but in your pocket," Sleight told Kehoe. "You keep them caps right with us." It was simple common sense. Put those blasting caps next to the pyrotol, hit one bad bump, and the two men would be blown to bits.[41]

During the drive back Kehoe mentioned that he'd be happy to pass along some of the explosive material. "If you know anybody that wants to buy it, they can get it for a little more than I paid for it," he told Sleight.

They unloaded the boxes in Kehoe's barn, said their good-byes, and Sleight went on his next errand, a ride to the local freight house where he needed to pick up a stove. It was late afternoon when Harry Barnard met Sleight there. They lifted the stove onto the truck bed, then headed over to Sleight's. "I haven't been home since this morning," Sleight told Barnard. "I have been down with Andrew Kehoe to get some pyrotol."

"I wish I had known that," Barnard said. "I would have sent for some."

Some time later, Sleight ran into another friend who said his brother needed explosives for stump blasting. Sleight suggested that the brother contact Kehoe. As it turned out, Kehoe said he didn't have any left.[42]

Eventually Kehoe didn't need Sleight or anyone else to drive him on errands. In February 1926, some seven years after moving to town, Kehoe finally acquired a machine of his own, a flatbed Ford truck, good transportation for a farmer.[43]

Still, considering his penny-pinching reputation, it seemed like an expensive purchase, particularly for a man who wasn't exactly getting rich in the farming business.

In the summer of 1926, Nellie Kehoe, always a quiet woman who seemingly lived in the shadow of her boisterous husband, developed serious health problems. She was hospitalized for a short while in the summer; soon she was plagued with a series of mind-numbing headaches, followed by severe coughing. Color drained from her face. Nellie lost weight off her medium-build frame. She was in and out of Saint Lawrence Hospital in Lansing throughout the fall and into the winter.[44] Doctors first thought it was tuberculosis, then decided it was asthma.[45] At home she rarely ventured out of the house, becoming something of a recluse to her already small social circle. A young woman was hired to help around the house as Nellie couldn't do much for herself.

Charlotte Howell, the wife of the Kehoe's neighbor Sydney Howell, was deeply concerned about the situation and often stopped by to check on Nellie. On one visit, the hired girl whisked Mrs. Howell to an upstairs room. Nellie Kehoe sat in the corner, pale, sickly, coughing, wheezing. Every breath, it seemed, was a painful struggle. Worried that her presence was too upsetting, Mrs. Howell offered to leave lest she upset Nellie. The feeling was mutual, albeit opposite: Mrs. Kehoe was more concerned that she might pass her illness on to Charlotte. "Mrs. Kehoe,"

Mrs. Howell said, "you know there is nothing in the world I wouldn't do for you."

"I know," Nellie responded.

But there was nothing she could do. As Charlotte Howell walked down the staircase, she heard the sounds of Nellie Kehoe's loud coughs following her every step.[46]

◆ ◆ ◆

A grove of trees, always a beautiful sight no matter what the season, was on the edge of Kehoe's farm. Over time it unofficially became known as Kehoe's Woods.

It was a plentiful source of firewood. Once, while Kehoe was working in the grove, a tree crashed through the foliage, bringing down heavy branches and landing with a magnificent thud.

Kehoe was hit, hit bad. He emerged from the woods, blood pouring down his face.

Unlike his fall in Saint Louis, this crack on the skull didn't knock Kehoe into a coma.[47]

◆ ◆ ◆

Buildings are like people, built of intricate parts and plumbing. When something goes wrong, it must be dealt with immediately lest a simple problem develop into something more complicated. No one knew that better than the school janitor, Frank Smith.

Smith wasn't sure, but in the fall of 1926 he had a feeling there was a leak in one of the basement pipes. While Superintendent Huyck shined a flashlight along the ceiling, Smith followed the length of pipe with his eye. Nothing. No leak, no rust, no loose joints.

He didn't notice something else in the ceiling that was out of place.[48]

Chapter 6

A GROWING STORM

Despite his reputation as the activist steward of public funds, Kehoe lacked any personal sense of fiscal responsibility. Up through March of 1921, he made regular payments on his mortgage and interest to the Lawrence Price Estate. And then: nothing.

April came and went. May slipped by. June, July, August. No payments. It continued through the rest of the year and into 1922. Not a word was said, not by the Price family or Joseph H. Dunnebacke, the attorney representing the estate. Finally a letter arrived from Kehoe stating that he couldn't make the payments. The estate granted him an extension. Another year passed, then another. Kehoe wrote another letter. Would he and Nellie be evicted? Again the answer was a calming no. By all means, the estate would be happy to work with Kehoe.

And still no payments. In August of 1925, Lawrence Price's estate released 60 percent of its legacy payments to the late man's heirs. Nellie Kehoe's share was twelve hundred dollars. The Kehoes arrived at Dunnebacke's office, collected their check, and left. Although Dunnebacke remained polite throughout, he was amazed that the couple never brought up the subject of their defaulted mortgage.[1]

The matter took another strange turn one month later. The probate judge overseeing Lawrence Price's estate received a letter from Nellie Kehoe. Enclosed was a card on which Nellie asked the judge to write down the appraised worth of the Kehoe property.[2]

And still no payments.

In March of 1926, Dunnebacke was bound by terms of the Lawrence Price Estate to provide Nellie Kehoe with another five hundred dollars. This time the attorney applied the money to payments on the house, sending the Kehoes a note explaining what he was doing with the small inheritance check. Nellie wrote back, thanking Dunnebacke and asking how much she and her husband owed on their mortgage. She also mentioned that Andrew was deeply involved with school board activities, but at some point they would like to come to Dunnebacke's office to discuss their debt.[3]

Instead, in the days following the school board debacle over Ruth Babcock, Kehoe contacted Kelly Searl, one of the best legal minds in the region. Searl, a former Circuit Court judge, had left the bench nearly ten years earlier to again practice law, entering into a partnership with his son William. Ultimately, William left private practice to become county prosecutor.

For now, Searl the elder agreed with Kehoe's argument that the executors had inappropriately diverted Nellie's inheritance check. Legally, the money had to go to Mrs. Kehoe. The executors of Lawrence Price's estate could not make decisions on Nellie's behalf without her consent.

Notice was sent to Dunnebacke and Richard Price, the estate executor, who had originally sold the property to Andrew and Nellie. They agreed to meet with Searl in the chambers of the probate judge, a man named McArthur.

It was assumed that the probate hearing, held in August of 1926, would be a simple matter during which the dispute would be solved through sound discussion and compromise between legal authorities. Instead, and to everyone's surprise, the Kehoes were there. They had not been notified of the time and place; apparently Kehoe had done some investigating. Dunnebacke was dismayed; he'd gone out of his way to help the Kehoes, particularly in light of Nellie's health, and felt they should leave the matter to be solved by legal parties. Yet the hearing continued with Kelly Searl's clients soaking in every word.

Dunnebacke thought it "peculiar" that the inheritance was in Nellie's name, the property deed in her husband's name, and the mortgage held by the couple. Legally, Nellie had the final decision about how to use her inheritance. Judge McArthur's findings were simple: yes, the Price estate had acted inappropriately, but applying the five hundred dollars to the mortgage would be in everyone's best interest.

Searl advised his clients to accept the decision. Nellie indicated that she liked the idea, but Kehoe disagreed. Polite but firm, he insisted that the money go to Nellie immediately; she could then decide how to use it without any legal intrusion.

Nellie acquiesced to her husband; they were issued a check for five hundred dollars.[4]

Two months passed without a word from the Kehoes. No payments. No agreements or offers made to alleviate the problem. Having exhausted all legal avenues, Dunnebacke decided to file a motion of foreclosure with the county sheriff, Bart Fox. He and his wife drove to Fox's office on a Saturday only to find that the sheriff was out. Rather than making the trip twice, Dunnebacke mailed his notice to the sheriff a few days later. That afternoon he ran into Nellie's sister, Elizabeth Price, and told her of the foreclosure suit. He assured her that this legal move was not an attempt to drive the Kehoes off the property; rather it was an attempt to coax them into negotiating a payment plan.

Elizabeth Price's face knotted. No, she told Dunnebacke, he mustn't file suit. Nellie's health was fragile; any added stress could have dire consequences.

Dunnebacke, a model of patience and empathy, agreed not to move ahead with the foreclosure. Long into the night he attempted to contact the sheriff. Unable to contact Fox, Dunnebacke sent a telegram.

> Have tried since five o'clock to reach your office by telephone. Don't serve Kehoe's summons until further instructions from me. Dunnebacke.

Unfortunately, the telegram didn't arrive quickly enough; a deputy had gone to the Kehoe residence with a notice of foreclosure. Kehoe came to the door and took the papers.[5] He looked them over, then regarded the man at the door.

"If it hadn't been for that three hundred dollar school tax, I might have paid off the mortgage," he said.[6]

◆ ◆ ◆

Every element of his life seemed to be waging war with Kehoe. The mortgage. Nellie's health. His political ambitions beaten down. And the fights, the constant fights on the school board, his anger toward Huyck growing. Kehoe's mind was on fire, taking him in different directions as he assessed the situation. His behavior, once considered eccentric and cantankerous, grew erratic.

Monty Ellsworth, who lived down the road from Kehoe, observed much of this firsthand. Ellsworth was something of a rascally figure himself, who tried his hand at various businesses: bartender, farmer, gas station owner. Although Ellsworth had something of a drinking problem and was plagued with asthma (in this he probably had some empathy with Nellie Kehoe), he was a friendly neighbor who often spoke with Kehoe.

What Kehoe had to say, however, was often odd. In the spring of 1925, Ellsworth bought a tenant house to be moved off Kehoe's property at a price of $250.00. Ellsworth offered $50.00 down on the building with the remainder to be paid on delivery day.

"No," Kehoe told Ellsworth, "I am selling it now because I want to use the money." Although not a standard way of doing business, Ellsworth agreed to Kehoe's unusual terms, paying full price before moving the building to his land. It's not clear whether Ellsworth knew of Kehoe's mortgage problems at the time.[7]

The two men often talked shop. In February of 1926 Ellsworth asked Kehoe if he was planning on attending a session during Farmers Week at Michigan State College. "No," Kehoe shot back. "They would just tell the farmers a lot of things that were impossible to do."

Kehoe continued, saying he had listened to one of the Farmers Week lecturers on the radio. "[The] speaker started in by telling what colleges he had been to and what countries he had been in. I shut that off and went to the telephone and called the college and asked them what in hell they wanted of a speaker who would just get up and brag about himself. That's the last time I'm going to listen to them this week."[8]

Another strange conversation stuck out in Ellsworth's mind. The weather had been up and down with bitter cold nights that froze farmland followed by warm daylight thaws.

"This is not good wheat weather," Ellsworth remarked to Kehoe.

Kehoe's response caught his neighbor off guard. "No," said Kehoe, "and I am glad of it. The farmers ought not to raise any more wheat until the country needed it badly. The damned fool farmers will never be any better off than they are now because if they do raise anything they will brag about it to everyone else." Take, for example, he continued, a northern Michigan farmer who had been at the 1926 Farmers Week. Why, this man had raised a double crop's worth of potatoes and what did this idiot do? He went down and bragged about it!

Again Philip Kehoe's voice echoed in his son's comments. A long time ago the father had argued that farmers should manage their output and set prices to control the market and guide their destinies. Now Kehoe repeated his father's ideas, yet there was something odd, something disturbing, about the way Kehoe stated his case.[9]

David Harte had similar thoughts about Kehoe's behavior. How could a man run an eighty-acre farm wearing a smoking jacket and puffing on cigars all day, he wondered. Why, Kehoe didn't even bother to harvest his corn or bring in a thresher to do the job. What was with that man, letting his crops rot in the fields?[10]

◆ ◆ ◆

In mid-November of 1926 Kehoe visited Lansing where he purchased two boxes of 40 percent Hercules dynamite. He went back a few days later to buy several blasting caps and two more boxes of 40 percent Hercules; he made additional trips for more blasting caps during that time as well. In December he made another trip to Lansing, buying himself a Winchester rifle and one hundred rounds of ammunition.[11]

◆ ◆ ◆

On December 31, as 1926 turned into 1927, Bath celebrated in typical fashion. The Community Hall was crowded with teens for a New Year's dance, which, of course, was overseen by a few adult chaperones.[12] Elsewhere in town friends gathered to mark Mrs. Artemus Clark's ninety-third birthday. The weather that night was typical of the season, with the temperature holding in the mid-twenties.[13]

Midnight struck. As couples kissed and people wished each other happy New Year, the celebrations were interrupted by loud *booms!* Massive explosions rocked the area as though Bath was under attack. A series of bright flashes lit up the Kehoe farmland. Then all was silent. A cloud of dust and smoke hung in the air.

It was unsettling for a quiet farm town, something for people to talk about. A few days later Harry Cushman ran into his friend Job Sleight and asked if he had heard any dynamite explosions on New Year's Eve.

"No," Job replied, "what of it?" Sleight apparently was the soundest sleeper in town.

"Kehoe shot off some New Year's night about midnight," Cushman told Sleight. "He was shooting off the old year."

"I guess so," said Sleight. It occurred to Sleight that he'd seen Kehoe walking around his farmhouse on January 1, looking upward with a careful eye. It was as though Kehoe wanted to be sure the chimney was still attached.

A few days later Sleight and his wife paid the Kehoes a visit. The foursome talked a bit, then Sleight asked about the holiday cacophony. "I heard you were shooting off dynamite New Year's Eve," he said.

"Yes," Kehoe replied. "I thought I would shoot some off. I set some out and wired it up and set it for twelve o'clock." He explained that a timing device was used to set off the explosives.

Kehoe laughed a little to himself. "I guess I jarred them up," he said.

As Sleight later recalled it, Mrs. Kehoe, who'd just been released from one of her many hospital stays, didn't say a word about her husband's New Year's festivities.[14]

◆ ◆ ◆

And still there were no payments on the mortgage.

In February of 1927 a professor at Michigan State College, looking to purchase a home for his father, made an offer for the property, the original twelve-thousand-dollar price Kehoe paid in 1920. Kehoe was hesitant about selling, but his feelings were quickly moot. The offer was withdrawn when the potential buyer decided the taxes on the land were exorbitant.[15]

The farm still generated interest even though the owners hadn't put it up for sale. A few weeks after the professor's offer fell through, a potential buyer asked Dunnebacke about the property; wisely the attorney decided to stay out of the situation, sending the man to Nellie's sisters. His reasoning was that the sisters knew Mrs. Kehoe best, which put them in a better position to discuss a potential sale. Again nothing came of the offer.

On March 31, Kehoe paid an unexpected visit to Dunnebacke's office. A third party was interested in buying the farm. As part of the sale, Kehoe was offered equity in an unnamed property and would have to sign an option agreement.

What did Dunnebacke think?

The attorney told Kehoe he "wasn't crazy about the deal." It would put Kehoe in a bad negotiating position. He would have to sign an option, whereas the buyer would not; additionally, there was little information on the second property for which Kehoe would be given equity.

Kehoe thanked Dunnebacke. It seemed like good advice, he said.

In mid-April Dunnebacke and Kehoe ran into each other downtown. The two men shook hands, made small talk.

What did you do about that deal, Dunnebacke asked.

The advice was good, Kehoe told him. He had decided not to sign the option.

It was a pleasant enough exchange. It appeared that any animosity between the two had evaporated. Dunnebacke was relieved; perhaps Kehoe was finally coming to his senses.

It was his last meeting with Andrew Kehoe.[16]

◆ ◆ ◆

Kehoe's duties as school board treasurer included dispensing employee checks. This was a task Kehoe engaged in with cynical relish. Every twenty days he'd roam the school hallways, going from classroom to classroom, giving each teacher a paycheck. In a cold voice and with an expressionless face, he would tell each recipient, "Well, it's another month."[17]

When it came to Huyck's salary, Kehoe's delivery was sporadic at best. He'd often "forget" to bring the paycheck to the superintendent's office.[18]

Obsessive frugality was one thing for a school board member. Contempt for the faculty and administration was another animal. Kehoe wasn't winning any friends among his peers.

Not that it bothered him any.

◆ ◆ ◆

As janitor, part of Frank Smith's job was to make sure all the doors were closed at nightfall. It was a simple enough task, never a problem at all. That changed in early spring when he saw something a little out of the ordinary.

The back door was split around the lock. It was an odd little break; Smith couldn't really tell how it had happened. Still, with a little effort the door closed.

In early May the lock stopped working altogether. As usual when it came to repairs, Kehoe was consulted. This time he couldn't do a thing, so the lock bracket was taken off its shock absorber and sent to Lansing for repairs.[19]

◆ ◆ ◆

Allen McMullen, a man of some sixty-nine years, enjoyed watching Kehoe install a lighting system on a neighbor's farm. It was something new, something different. McMullen and Kehoe exchanged pleasantries, just idle chitchat between two men. One evening Kehoe made McMullen an offer.

"Have you any use for a horse?" asked Kehoe.

"I don't know," McMullen replied. It had been a few years since he had had a horse on his farm. "I expect I could use one once in a while."

"Well," Kehoe said, "There is two horses over in the barn tearing the barn down. Come on over and get one."

Kehoe asked what McMullen would give him for the horse; McMullen said he wasn't interested in buying the animal. They let it go at that.

A few days later Kehoe arrived at the McMullen farm, proffering horse and harness. The animal, named Kit, was blind in one eye.

Regardless of the horse's condition, the gift caught McMullen by surprise. "This is pretty nice to have somebody wait on you like that," he told Kehoe.

"Oh, I don't mind that," Kehoe said.

McMullen's sister happened to be at the house; would Kehoe like her to drive him back home?

"No," Kehoe told McMullen, "I don't mind walking back." The whole visit, from beginning to end, didn't last more than five minutes.

Two nights later McMullen was having supper at a mutual friend's house when Kehoe stopped by on some business. Once again Nellie was in the hospital, and the friend, a man by the name of Weed, insisted that Kehoe stay for dinner.

It was a clear evening, a nice time to be outside before a meal. McMullen and Kehoe sat on the porch for a few minutes, talking shop. Then, almost as an afterthought, Kehoe reached into his pocket, pulled out a typewritten piece of paper, and handed it to McMullen.

"What is this?" McMullen asked.

"Read it," Kehoe told him.

"I can't read it," McMullen said. "I haven't got my glasses." Kehoe offered to oblige.

He read the paper nonchalantly.

It was a bill of sale for the horse.

May 4. 1927, Received from Allen McMullen
One hundred twenty dollars in
full payment for one bay mare,
ten years old, blind in left eye,
weight 1800 pounds. Named Kit.
$120.00. A. P. Kehoe.

This was the first Kehoe told him the horse was not a gift but a sale. Money was not asked for until now.

McMullen was at a loss for words.

Not knowing what the legalities were in this situation, McMullen held on to the horse for a few more days. Did the bill of sale mean he was responsible even though he never asked to buy the horse? Finally he drew one conclusion: he must go to Kehoe and say he would return the animal.

Although he knew Kehoe was spending every morning in Lansing visiting Nellie in the hospital, McMullen took a chance and went over to the house on May 7 around eight o'clock. He saw Kehoe's Ford in the yard; apparently he was home. McMullen went to the backdoor and knocked. No answer. He went around to the front and knocked on that door, again no answer.

McMullen dawdled a bit in front of the house. Maybe the man was just sleeping in.

Finally he walked across the road to the David Harte place. Did they know if Kehoe was home?

"I saw a light there late in the night," Lulu Harte told him.

David Harte invited McMullen in to use the telephone and call Kehoe. "You might rout him up," Harte said.

There was no answer. McMullen visited with the Hartes a while, then decided to try knocking on Kehoe's door again. Still no answer. He sat down on the steps, sat there the better part of an hour, wondering what was going on inside. McMullen tossed over various scenarios in his mind, none of them pretty. Maybe Kehoe's gone and hung himself, he thought, though there was no reason to believe this was the case. Finally, McMullen figured he ought to round up some neighbors. Something was seriously wrong; if Kehoe was hurt he would surely need help.

But just once more McMullen tried the door, knocking as hard as he could. After a moment, he heard something inside. Kehoe was coming down the stairs, alive and apparently well. Wearing just pants and his bedroom slippers, Kehoe opened the door and greeted his unexpected visitor.

"What is the matter?" McMullen asked. "Are you going to kill yourself sleeping?"

Bemused, Kehoe gave a sly grin. "It wouldn't be a bad way to die, would it?" he said.

"Probably no," said McMullen. Kehoe invited McMullen in. The two men talked a while, McMullen hemming and hawing with excuses about why he didn't want the horse. Kehoe was surprised but conciliatory, offering a glass of cider to his guest. He went down to the basement to fetch the cider, then sat back down with McMullen. "Now you sit tight," Kehoe said. Kehoe said he had to feed his other horse and then would drive McMullen home.

McMullen declined the offer, saying he didn't mind walking back. Kehoe insisted. McMullen downed his cider, then followed Kehoe out to the barn. The horse was fed. Kehoe walked over to his machine and again offered to take McMullen home.

"No, go on and get your breakfast," McMullen said. "You are going to town. Go on, I can walk home."

"No, I ain't going to get any breakfast until I get to town," Kehoe said. "I won't be going down for an hour or so. I have got to shave." Finally, McMullen acquiesced. After dropping McMullen at home, Kehoe quickly turned around and headed back to his farm.

A few days later, Kehoe called McMullen, saying he was going to town, and asked if McMullen's sister would like a lift. That she did, and McMullen thought this would be a ripe time to bring the horse back. When he was about a quarter mile from his destination, McMullen saw Kehoe coming down the road. Kehoe appeared surprised. The two men talked a bit, then Kehoe told McMullen, "I will go back and help you put the horse in the barn." Again he offered to take McMullen home once they were done.

As they put the horse in its stable, Kehoe looked at McMullen. "Al," he said, "You made a mistake by not keeping that horse over there."

McMullen chose not to reply.

Kehoe drove McMullen back to the road. McMullen's sister was there, waiting for Kehoe, so McMullen decided to walk back to his farm.

From start to finish, the whole episode was strange and a little unsettling. Allen McMullen had no more dealings with Andrew Kehoe.[20]

Throughout the fall and into winter and spring Nellie Kehoe's health grew worse. Blinding headaches, the constant rasping cough, a body wracked by ill health. There seemed to be no end to it. She was constantly in and out Saint Lawrence Hospital. Alone during those times, Kehoe usually ate his meals in town. He often drove to Lansing to visit his wife in the hospital.

David Harte sometimes saw Kehoe's truck at night coming home from what Harte assumed was a trip to Saint Lawrence Hospital. He always knew when Kehoe was out; the man never shut his garage door when he left and always closed it up tight when he returned. Generally speaking, Kehoe's trips weren't late; he usually came back between eight and nine o'clock.

In mid-April, Harte noticed that Kehoe's trips were on the increase and he often had boxes covered with some kind of tarp in the bed of his truck. Kehoe never said a word about any of this.[21]

◆ ◆ ◆

In late April or early May Kehoe bought a hotshot battery from an automotive and radio supply shop in Lansing. A hotshot battery, commonly used as an alternative to the hand crank when starting a Model T Ford, was made up of four one-and-a-half-volt dry cell batteries, each cell being about two and a half inches around and between six to seven inches long. The combined voltage of the cells was about six volts, enough to fire up a car engine or any other sort of device that needed a handy electrical spark. Kehoe also purchased a new set of tires for his truck.[22]

◆ ◆ ◆

In early May, as Frank Smith made his rounds in the school basement he noticed something funny. There were a couple of trapdoors down there, each about eighteen inches square. One of them was open. Come to think of it, this wasn't the first time he'd seen that. Seems maybe he'd found both trapdoors open two or three times before.

Strange. He hadn't left them open as far as he could remember.[23]

◆ ◆ ◆

Payday. Ward Kyes said good morning to Kehoe and took his check, just like always. He was about to put it in his pocket when his foot slipped off the clutch. Ward jumped back so the bus wouldn't roll, accidentally dropping his paycheck in the process.

Kehoe watched the piece of paper float to the ground. "You better keep that," he told Ward. "That may be the last you will ever get."

He's good-natured this morning, Ward thought, as he laughed at the little joke. "Are you going broke?" Ward asked.

"I guess not," Kehoe said.[24]

◆ ◆ ◆

A year or so earlier Kehoe had proudly showed Monty Ellsworth his Winchester bolt-action rifle, a real beauty of a gun. Ellsworth mentioned at the time that he had a rifle he never used; maybe he and Kehoe could target shoot sometime. "That's a fine idea," his neighbor replied, giving Ellsworth an open invitation to come anytime he wanted.

Ellsworth, a man with many ideas, planned to open a gas station on the road in front of his house. It made potentially good business sense; with the increase in automobiles in the area, people would need gasoline. Who better to buy it from than their neighbor?

Come Thursday, May 12, Ellsworth was working in his yard, getting things ready for construction. When Kehoe came over to chat, Ellsworth took a break.

They didn't talk about much, just general conversation between neighbors. Kehoe reminded Ellsworth that they had never got together for the promised target practice session. Ellsworth explained the obvious; he'd been up to his armpits in work. But would Kehoe like to come over the next day? "Sure," Kehoe replied.

He promptly arrived on Friday, May 13, at 8:30 a.m., gun and pasteboard targets in hand. The two men nailed the targets to a board and set them up one hundred yards away.

Ellsworth fired off three rounds, one a bull's-eye, one close to center, and one wildly off target. Kehoe had better aim, hitting one bull's-eye and two shots close to center. The men moved the targets fifty feet closer, exchanged guns, and again fired three rounds apiece. Once more Kehoe displayed a steady hand and excellent aim, beating Ellsworth nicely. Ellsworth gave Kehoe his Winchester back and tried firing with his own gun once more.

Three, four, five, six times they shot. Kehoe's aim was tight, besting his opponent in each contest. Ellsworth stood in awe of his neighbor's talents.

When it was over Ellsworth walked with Kehoe back to the truck. There was something in the back, a crate of some kind about two feet long and a foot wide. The box was partially filled with rifle shells, maybe a thousand or so by Ellsworth's guess.

A week later Ellsworth wondered how Kehoe had maintained such cool during their target shooting considering all the man had weighing on his mind.[25]

◆ ◆ ◆

On Saturday, May 14 a construction crew working on a bridge near Bath reported a large quantity of dynamite was missing.[26]

◆ ◆ ◆

Looking across the road, Lulu Harte noticed Kehoe loading up his truck. There was something odd about Kehoe's cargo. It looked like old wheels and assorted scrap, not the everyday items farmers normally packed into their machines.

"You don't suppose he is junking his tools?" Lulu asked her husband.[27]

◆ ◆ ◆

A good deal of work was necessary before Ellsworth could open his filling station. In the process of setting up a temporary air compressor, Ellsworth realized he needed some pipe fittings.

Kehoe was so handy; just a year or so ago he'd helped Ellsworth with a troublesome boiler. Ellsworth figured his neighbor might have some pipe fittings to attach the compressor. It was the right assumption. They talked a bit about the work Ellsworth was doing on the filling station and an upcoming mechanical adjustment that would be necessary. "I'm doing it in about a week or so," Ellsworth explained.

"When you get ready to do that," Kehoe said, "come down if you need any tools. Yes, and I will help you."

Ellsworth thought this was a nice neighborly offer.[28]

Saturday happened to be the Kehoes' fifteenth wedding anniversary. With Nellie in the hospital once more, Kehoe didn't do much in the way of celebration. Rather, he spent the afternoon settling accounts with some of his creditors. Paying the mortgage was not on this list.[29]

On Sunday, May 15, he planned to pick Nellie up from the hospital, explaining to her sisters that she would be staying in Jackson with some friends. But someone from the hospital called that morning; it was a rainy day and would he mind coming tomorrow so as not to aggravate Nellie's lung condition. Kehoe agreed, saying he would check Nellie out of the hospital on Monday, May 16.[30]

♦ ♦ ♦

David Harte heard through the grapevine that Kehoe wanted to sell one of his horses. He contacted a friend in Lansing, a fellow by the name of Seymour Champion, who was interested in acquiring a horse. Champion stopped by Harte's house on Monday afternoon and inquired about the animal. "Don't think Kehoe's in," Harte said. Champion disagreed, saying he'd just seen Kehoe carrying a bundle of straw into his henhouse.

When the two men went over, Kehoe was indeed working in the chicken coop. He came out to greet his visitors.

Harte introduced Champion, then asked how Nellie was feeling. Much better, Kehoe told him, saying that his wife was in Lansing with her sisters. Kehoe went into the farmhouse to wash his hands. After cleaning up, the bargaining began.

It was the same horse Kehoe had offered McMullen. Kehoe said he'd sell Champion the horse for a hundred dollars. No, said the potential buyer; it was too high a price for an old, one-eyed horse.

As Kehoe and Champion haggled back and forth, Harte noticed a pair of thin copper wires on the ground. The wires reached from the henhouse to a toolshed and back to the henhouse. Looks like Kehoe is preparing for the Consumers Power men, bringing electrical wiring to the area, Harte thought.

Ultimately there was no deal on the horse. Champion later told Harte that he'd have bought the horse for sixty dollars. He also got the feeling that Kehoe was a "funny man."

Harte, long used to Kehoe's eccentricities, didn't see anything out of the ordinary in his neighbor's behavior that day.[31]

♦ ♦ ♦

Late in the afternoon, Kehoe picked up his wife. They spent the evening with Nellie's sisters in Lansing. The Kehoes were jovial company, happy that Nellie was out of the hospital. When the visit was over, the couple bade the Price sisters good-bye and went home to Bath.[32]

After the Kehoes returned to the farm, the telephone rang. It was Blanche Hart, the fifth-grade teacher. Having heard that Nellie was out of the hospital, she was calling to see how Nellie was feeling.

"She is getting along fine," Kehoe told Hart. "I have got her home here with me, and she is fussing around."

Hart thought that was good news, what with Nellie having been sick for so long.[33]

On Tuesday, May 17, a few days after their shooting contest, Kehoe stopped by Ellsworth's place. "I like that rifle of yours," Kehoe said. "Will you give me twenty-five dollars difference for that rifle of mine?"

Kehoe's offer took Ellsworth by surprise. "No," he told Kehoe. "I wouldn't give that much difference because I have no use for them." Ellsworth suggested giving a ten-dollar difference, a counteroffer Kehoe turned down. "That gun cost me fifty dollars, and they didn't have the sights I wanted," Kehoe said, adding that he had paid an extra eleven dollars for a special gun sight from a Detroit company.

No deal was made. Kehoe went home.[34]

◆ ◆ ◆

The end of school year always meant fun for the children; this year's classes were no exception. Bernice Sterling, the first-grade teacher, telephoned Kehoe. She asked if she could have a picnic with her students in the grove on the edge of Kehoe's farm.

"When are you going to have the picnic?" Kehoe asked her.

"Thursday," she said.

In retrospect Sterling felt Kehoe's response was both forthright and enigmatic. "Well," he told her, "if you're going to have a picnic, you'd better have it right away."[35]

◆ ◆ ◆

In the afternoon, as David Harte was driving his hay-filled wagon over to his son's place, he heard a horn behind him. This wasn't unusual, particularly in a town like Bath, where horses and wagons shared the road with trucks and automobiles.

The machine swung around Harte's wagon. Harte recognized his neighbor. Kehoe continued down the road, raising his hand in silent greeting.[36]

◆ ◆ ◆

One of the Price sisters called the Kehoe residence to see how Nellie was doing. There was no answer.

They heard from Kehoe that evening. "Have you been trying to get us on the telephone?" he asked. "Yes," was the reply, expressing concern about Nellie.

"Nellie is over to Jackson," Kehoe said. "She was lonesome here, and we have some friends by the name of Vost who we used to know at Tecumseh, and it occurred to me to take Nellie over there because I thought it would be a good thing for her.

"I am to go back for her on Thursday," he added, and then hung up.[37]

Come evening, David Harte saw something a little odd across the road. Andrew Kehoe's arms were full of straw as he walked into his hen-house. Wasn't he doing the same thing yesterday when Harte and Champion came to see him about the horse? Harte knew Kehoe had no birds; he'd sold his brood some time ago. Why would he spend so much time filling the coop with straw?

Maybe he's going to start chicken farming again, Harte thought.[38]

◆ ◆ ◆

Fordney Hart, a freshman at Bath Consolidated, finally was leaving school at 8:30 p.m. Although it was well past the end of the school day, the building was bustling with adults attending a Parent-Teacher Association meeting where Fordney had performed as part of a small orchestral ensemble.[39]

Someone was in front of the school. He wasn't doing anything in particular, just standing, looking at the building. Fordney thought this person looked familiar.

The teenager caught a glimpse of the man's gold front teeth. Fordney recognized him. He was always in and out of the school, that handy guy who had solved the bee problem and did other odd jobs.

Andrew Kehoe. That was the man's name. Now Fordney knew exactly who he was. Every once in a while, Fordney's parents went to play cards over at a neighbor's. Card games were boring to the teenager; instead he would drop by the Kehoe farm. Kehoe had a radio set he'd let Fordney play with now and again. Yes, that definitely was the same man now standing there in the dark. And wasn't it just a month ago that Kehoe had dynamited some old stumps out of a relative's fields?[40]

The two apparently never acknowledged each other. Fordney headed home. Kehoe remained in front of the school, alone.[41]

Chapter 7

ELECTRICITY

The morning of May 18, 1927, began with electricity. Lightning hovered over Bath during an early morning rainstorm, piercing the sky with occasional crackling bolts. It was a good spring shower, the kind that cleanses the land and refreshes crops.

As day broke, electricity was crossing the sky in a different form. Linemen, resembling steeplejacks shimmying up church spires, climbed wooden poles planted along Clark Road. Ropey black wires were strung along the tops of the poles, bearing the promise of cheap and plentiful power on demand courtesy of Michigan's Consumers Power Company. This promised an enormous change for the rural town. Some homes—such as Kehoe's—used a generator for electricity. Public buildings—including the Bath Consolidated School—also used generators. There was a public generator in town as well for some of the other buildings, although it wasn't reliable. That was the problem with generators. Even the best of them had to be nursed like newborn kittens, constantly fed and watched over to make sure they maintained healthy purrs.

The men on the poles represented a new dawn. The instantaneous bright lights of the Roaring Twenties were—at last—coming to Bath.

Beneath the Consolidated School building, electricity was in limbo. The well pump, which provided water to the school, was acting up. Frank Smith was expecting the repairman, a Mr. Harrington, but didn't know what time he was coming.[1]

Harrington was a real character. He only had one arm, and for fun he liked to grab a student now and again, hold the victim between his stump and rib cage, and give a wicked head rub using his only hand.[2]

Figuring it would be a few hours before Harrington arrived to fix the pump, Smith didn't want to fire up the generator just yet. The school would have to make do without power this morning.[3]

The near-future of Kehoe's farm was dependent on electricity as well, though it would have to wait a little longer to unleash. There was business to attend to first. Shortly after daybreak, Kehoe loaded a package into his truck and drove to town. It was urgent that the package—an old packing crate cut down to size, loaded with some kind of material, and sealed tight—be sent this morning to Clyde B. Smith, a Lansing insurance man. The two had a working relationship through the school board: Smith's agency was responsible for the six-thousand-dollar surety bond on Bath Consolidated, which Kehoe had posted after he was elected treasurer.

From his farm it was a quick drive into town. Kehoe parked his machine in front of the post office. The building had yet to open for the day. With no desire to waste time, Kehoe carried his package over to the nearby railway depot and arranged for a morning delivery to Lansing. The box could be sent express rail via the next train to Laingsburg, and from there it would go out on the first train to Lansing. The stencil noting the box's original contents apparently made little impression on D. B. Huffman, the railway agent.

The simple black letters read, "High Explosives. Dangerous."[4]

Albert Detluff was also in town at this early hour, having just picked up some duck's eggs from a nearby farm. He knew about Smith's situation with the pump and wanted to check out the problem for himself. Seeing Kehoe walking to his truck, Detluff called out and drove his machine over to his fellow school board trustee.

The two men engaged in idle talk, the kind of banter that one takes for granted in the moment but becomes strangely significant in stark hindsight. Detluff asked Kehoe when the next board meeting was. Either the nineteenth or the twentieth, Kehoe replied. Detluff mentioned that there were problems with the well at the school and would Kehoe mind joining him to take a quick look?

Kehoe got in his truck and drove to the schoolhouse as Detluff followed in his own car. When they arrived, Kehoe told Detluff he remembered that the school board meeting was this Friday, the twentieth. As they walked into the building, Kehoe checked his watch: 8:25. It was almost time for school to begin, he pointed out, probably not enough time to look at the pump. No, Detluff insisted, the time was really 7:25. Kehoe kept his watch on Eastern Time and Detluff on Central, which was how the school clocked its day. "We have plenty of time," Detluff said.

Kehoe hesitated for a moment. "Yes, we have," he replied.

The two looked over the pump, reached no conclusion, and moved on to the generator. Smith, who had been at the school since six that morning, was fiddling with the oil burners. More small talk rattled through the air as Detluff and Smith theorized about what the problem with the pump could be.

Kehoe, seemingly remote just a moment before, suddenly came to life. "You know, I'm in an awful hurry!" he snapped. He abruptly exited the generator room, leaving the problem for Detluff and Smith to solve.

They ignored Kehoe's outburst and concentrated on the generator and pump. "If I thought Mr. Harrington would be down here to fix this within a couple of hours, I wouldn't start this up," Smith told Detluff.

"Let's go out and see if we can see him," the trustee replied.

The two men went outside to see if the repairman was in sight. Detluff noticed that Kehoe's machine was gone.[5]

◆ ◆ ◆

At the Cushman house, seven-year-old Ralph was almost ready to leave for school. This was no easy task. With summer vacation beginning in just two days, it was hard for the energetic boy to contain his excitement. How would he be able to sit still for his teacher when his thoughts inevitably were drifting to the school-free days of June? Ralph was poised on three months devoted to nothing but his one great love, baseball. Why, even before this day started, Ralph had managed to get in a little baseball time. Chances were he'd think of nothing else until the school bell set him free at day's end.

Finally, he gave in to the inevitable. Just before leaving the house, he paused. "Good-bye, Mama," he called out. "I'll be good!"[6]

His older sister Josephine, who had six years on her brother, walked Ralph to school. When they arrived she offered to sit with him. Josephine knew what a bashful kid Ralph was, and maybe he'd like some company until it was time to go to class.

"No!" Ralph said. Nothing could be more embarrassing than having the other children see him with his older sister.

"Okay," Josephine replied, "that's all right. I'll see you at lunchtime."[7]

Like he did every morning, Robert Harte, an energetic nine year old, fed the chickens on the family farm. This was no small task since the Hartes had a brood of around twenty-two hundred birds. When he finished, Robert grabbed his lunch bucket and took off for school. His mother, Florence, looked fondly after him as he ran off. "See you later, Mom!" he yelled over his shoulder.[8]

Over at the Bauerle house, Henry and his wife Hertha were getting ready to go shoe shopping in Lansing with their two oldest children, Herbert and Esther. Arnold, their mathematically minded third grader, desperately wanted to join the family. He'd been laid up with whooping cough for some time but finally was feeling like his regular self. A drive to Lansing certainly was more promising than a day in school. But no, his parents decided, Arnold had missed enough classes because of his illness. Go to school today. There would be more trips to Lansing.[9]

At the Hart residence, twelve-year-old Iola kissed her mother good-bye as she did every morning. "Don't worry if I don't come home at noon," she teased. "You know I have to write tests this morning and I might faint away."

Lilacs were blooming. Iola picked a bouquet on the way to school.[10]

So it was throughout the area. At the Bergan home. The Chapmans, the Claytons, the Ewings, the McFarrens, the MacDonalds, the Smiths, the Witchells, and the Zimmermans. The Babcocks, the Burnetts, the Englands, the Fultons. The Hobarts, the Komms, the Kings. The Perrones, the Reasoners, the Reeds, the Sages. The Stebletons, the Wilsons, and the Zavistoskis. Scenes of mundane, utter normalcy played out in countless ways.

With the school generator out, Principal Floyd Huggett relied on a gong bell attached to a chain to call the students to order. Only twenty-six years old and with the school for the past four years, Huggett undertook his duties with the professionalism of an administrator twice his age. He rang the bell at 8:30 Central Time, then went to the Bath Methodist Church next door, where the commencement was scheduled to take place the next day, to meet some students for a graduation rehearsal. Seniors were in the midst of final examinations, so not all of the young people were in class that morning. The early morning hour was perfect for fine-tuning last minute details.

Huggett met Bertha Kumm and Thelma Cressman. Thelma read three stanzas of a poem she was going to deliver during the ceremony. The reading was good, but Huggett had some suggestions for her delivery. He started giving Thelma his thoughts.[11]

Arthur Woodman, Donald Ewing, Charley Haveling, and William Robb, senior boys, gathered in front of the school. Free from the worries of exams for the moment, they grabbed a baseball and played an impromptu game.

Charley was pitching to Arthur, who stood about twenty feet away. The throw went high, sending Arthur on a wild chase. He was determined to catch the ball.[12]

Ten-year-old Lee Mast, a fifth grader, didn't want to go to school that morning. His hip hurt for some reason; he must have slept on it funny. That excuse didn't wash with his mother, and off to school he went.

His teacher, Blanche Hart, asked Lee to run an errand for her. Any excuse to get out of class was a good one, and he gladly took on this special assignment. As he walked down the hall, Lee felt a nice breeze wafting into the building through the windows.[13]

Leona Gutekunst, the second-grade teacher, was just about finished reading a story to her class. Miss Gutekunst had a real gift for reading aloud. Stories seemed to come to life whenever she opened a book. Some of the second graders were seated at a round table with Miss Gutekunst; the others spilled onto the floor at her feet.

After completing the tale, Miss Gutekunst told the children it was time for something else. No, her students begged, just one more story, please. Their minds certainly weren't on their lessons, what with summer vacation about to start. Well, why not? One more story wouldn't hurt. For the moment, the students wouldn't have to return to their desks along the west side of the classroom.[14]

Willis Cressman, now in the tenth grade, thought he'd go to the school library and catch up on some reading. A teacher stood in the doorway and refused to let Cressman in. He was puzzled by this, but figured he'd go to the assembly room study hall and get things done there instead.[15]

Having dropped off Ralph at school, Josephine Cushman headed to the woods to pick wildflowers with some of her girlfriends. The woods just south of the school near the cemetery, were blooming with wildflowers and lilies. Josephine had received a B in deportment class, the study of manners and personal conduct, and as a result she didn't have to take any final exams. Now freshman year was done, and it felt great to be free from school for the summer.

Besides, it was a wonderful morning to pick flowers.[16]

Carlton Hollister, a fifth grader, and his classmates normally met on the first floor in Mrs. Hart's classroom. This morning was different. Because the sixth grade needed to take a geography exam it was decided that the older class would switch rooms with the fifth graders since Mrs. Hart's classroom was more conducive to testing. The fifth graders marched through the hallway in single file, passing their sixth-grade peers on the stairway.

Now resituated, Carlton took a seat in the center of the second-floor classroom. Naturally curious to see whose seat he had, he lifted the desk lid and pulled out a book. It belonged to Galen Hart, a good friend of Carlton's. The two boys often played together and were in the same church Sunday school class, too.[17]

◆ ◆ ◆

Beneath the north wing of the school, in a quiet nook in the basement, a small alarm clock ticked away. When the hands reached 8:45 a wire connected to the clock set off a spark. The spark started a chain reaction, firing electricity along a series of thin wires. Electrons raced along these preset pathways, careening along lines rigged throughout the basement.

Throughout their journey, the electrons heated the wires. At the end of each wire were blasting caps. The hot current ignited the blasting caps, sending more electrons into caches of dynamite and pyrotol.

Electrons smashed into each other with unrelenting fury. The minuteness of the particles belied their energy. On this bright May morning, a carefully planned trail of electricity unleashed an explosion of spectacular proportions beneath the north wing of the Bath Consolidated School.

◆ ◆ ◆

At about 8:45, in her henhouse tending to the family chickens, Lulu Harte heard a loud *thump* on the roof. She went outside to see what had happened, then heard what she instantly thought was a gunshot coming from the Kehoe property across the road.

She had seen Kehoe drive his machine off the property around seven or so that morning. Now Lulu saw smoke curling and billowing from the roof of Kehoe's corncrib. In a moment, flames licked the structure.

Lulu ran to find her husband. Kehoe's corncrib is on fire, she hastily told him. They raced to the front and saw that Kehoe's barn was ablaze as well, flames ripping through the building. Smoke, thick as fog, was pouring from the Kehoe house. The Hartes heard more gunshot noises blasting inside the home.

"Don't go over there!" cried David. "He certainly set it himself."[18]

◆ ◆ ◆

After Harrington arrived, Smith took him down to the school basement. They entered the small pump house, and Harrington began his work.

The two men went at it for about fifteen minutes. Then, without warning, an enormous roar sounded throughout the cellar. The force of it threw Harrington against the wall.

He struggled to get his bearings. He could see Smith trying to regain his footing. "For God's sake," Smith said, "what happened?"[19]

No matter how rock steady a building is, when met with the right amount of force it will collapse like a flimsy house of cards. On April 19, 1995, using a crude bomb made of ammonium nitrate, an agricultural fertilizer, and nitromethane, a highly volatile gasoline, Timothy McVeigh easily blew off the front of the Murrah Federal Building in Oklahoma City. The morning of September 11, 2001, terrorists using hijacked airplanes, fat

Fig. 4. *(Photograph by Fred A. Stevens.)*

with jet fuel, as missiles, effectively laid to waste the Twin Towers of the World Trade Center in New York City. These edifices, seemingly mighty structures, proved to be incredibly fragile.

So it was, too, on this morning under the north wing of the Bath Consolidated School, a building meant to last for generations. Dynamite and pyrotol combined in a powerful ball of energy. This forced the walls of the north wing upward about four feet. They fell back to earth, collapsing outward with a crash of wood, glass, plaster, and iron. The roof of the building slammed down onto the crumbling walls. A cloud of dust hovered above the ruins.[20] For a moment there was silence. And then a cacophony of screams.

◆　◆　◆

The western wall of Leona Gutekunst's classroom blasted into the room, smashing onto the empty desks. Had she not agreed to read one more tale to the children they would have been crushed beneath the collapsing rubble. "That story saved their lives," she later realized.[21]

Fig. 5. Hazel Weatherby.
*(Courtesy of the Bath
School Museum.)*

Bernice Sterling, the first-grade teacher, felt a sudden eruption as though a powerful earthquake had hit the classroom. She rode the floor as it shot into the air a few feet. Her students, who only moments before had been marching around the room for morning exercises, were instantly hurled like rag dolls, slamming into walls, crashing out of windows.[22]

Throughout the rest of building walls shook and floors buckled. In the assembly room, where Superintendent Emory Huyck was giving exams to seniors, light globes on the ceiling swung wildly. One broke loose and crashed to the floor.[23]

Windows of nearby homes were blown out. The blast sounded throughout the farmlands of Bath Township, and continued to echo for miles beyond. On several farms, it was later said, horses terrified by the exploding roar broke loose from their plows and scattered.

Mrs. LaHall Warner, a widow who lived just a block from Bath Consolidated, was putting a new curtain on her front porch window. She heard a powerful noise rock the air; a moment later she was pelted with glass.

Immediately, she ran outside. In horror she watched as the roof collapsed onto the remains of the school's north wing.[24]

Willitt Whitney, a sixty-six-year-old retiree, stood on top of a chair in his kitchen, washing the woodwork over the door frame. There was a roar from down the street. The chair rocked against the noise, sending Whitney hard onto the floor. "My God, what is that?" he said. Mrs. Whitney, already out the door, cried out that something had happened at the schoolhouse.[25]

Debris rained down on the classroom of twenty-one-year-old Hazel Weatherby, the third- and fourth-grade teacher. In a desperate, instinctive move, she reached out to shield her students. She pulled two children into her arms.

As Arthur Woodman reached for the falling baseball, he heard a tremendous sound. The force of the noise knocked him to the ground. He looked up to see the school roof caving in. It collapsed with a roar, engulfing the air with thick plaster dust. Through the dust, Arthur saw the crushed remains of the building and the forms of small children helplessly trapped in the rubble. Their screams hurtled through the foggy dust.[26]

Two boilers, suspended from the basement ceiling, were wrenched loose from their supports. They fell hard, closing off any connection between the north and south sections of the school. They may also have loosened some wires planted in the ceiling.[27]

The school roof crashed down on Carlton Hollister and his fifth-grade classmates. The second-floor classroom smashed down onto the sixth graders below. Had the two grades not switched classrooms just minutes earlier, their places would have been reversed.[28]

The blast heaved Sylvester Barnard, a fifteen-year-old sophomore, through a window. He landed with a thud. His body ached, but he managed to get up.

Bodies were strewn throughout the area. Some dead, some dying, some broken and wracked with unbearable pain.

It was too much to comprehend. Sylvester's eyes fluttered as he passed out.[29]

The inkwell on Willis Cressman's study hall desk flew up to the ceiling like a bullet. The building shook around the teenager; it felt like he was rising right up into the air.

For some unknown reason, Cressman later recalled, he didn't hear a thing. But the sight of that flying inkwell stayed with him for years.[30]

Ada Belle Dolton, a fifth grader, was knocked out of her desk. It didn't hurt; instead it felt like she was floating. Above her she could see her classmates and their desks hurtling through space. Through the spaces in between, Ada Belle glimpsed rays of sunshine.[31]

Principal Huggett felt the church rock. Pews tipped over as the floor rolled. Huggett grabbed a nearby desk to steady himself. Once he got his bearings, he, Bertha, and Thelma ran out of the building. Huggett saw an enormous cloud of dust, specks of plaster and dirt hovering around what remained of the north wing of the school.[32]

Evelyn Paul, the home economics teacher, heard a deafening blast and then saw an intense flash of light. A sharp sensation burned through her shoulder as a splinter of wood shot into her flesh. Plaster rained down, filling the room with powdery dust, and in a moment all was dark.

"What is it?" she heard students cry.

Paul opened her eyes. Through a window, penetrating the thick dust, she saw a beam of light.[33]

Cleo Clayton, an eight year old, leaped through a window, hit the ground, and ran to the front lawn of the school. For the moment, he was safe.

Seventeen-year-old Perry Hart, was in town running an errand for his mother. He'd dropped out of school some time before; the classroom just wasn't the place for Perry.

He heard the noise and felt the ground shake under his feet. He looked toward the sound. Something had happened at Bath Consolidated. He ran toward the school. His three sisters, Iola, Vivian, and Elva, and his brother Percy were inside.[34]

In the woods, Josephine Cushman heard a huge *boom!* It shook the trees and rattled the branches. The noise sounded like it came from the direction of the schoolhouse.

She and her friends quickly headed back to the building. As they passed a gas station on the corner, the owner shouted to them, "Hurry up! The school has blown up!"[35]

Fresh from his dealings with Smith and Kehoe, Albert Detluff started the workday at his blacksmith shop. This morning an automobile was hoisted in the air while an employee worked on the engine. Detluff went upstairs to attend to business.

At 8:45 an enormous boom sounded through the building. Detluff immediately ran downstairs. The hoist must have given way, sending the machine crashing to the floor. "What is going on down here?" he called out. No one answered. The building seemed to have emptied in the wake of the noise.

Detluff went outside, ran around the building, and then came back to the front. There was a man there now, screaming an alarm.

"The schoolhouse is blowed up!" the stranger shouted.[36]

Detluff immediately thought of his daughter Marcia who was in a home economics class that morning.

◆ ◆ ◆

On his farm west of town, Job Sleight worked on his morning chores. His head was throbbing; He was fighting off a bad cold with little success. "My head feels like I stepped into a hole," he thought. But, headache or no headache, chores had to be completed.

His head boomed once more. This was no headache pain; he instantly knew that something nearby had exploded. Maybe it was the men from Consumers Power blasting holes to set the new roadside poles. No, he realized, it was probably his neighbor Andrew Kehoe blowing off pyrotol, maybe ripping old tree stumps loose from his fields.

Sleight looked in the direction of Kehoe's farm. Nothing appeared to be out of the ordinary.

A woman appeared on the road, running as though the world depended on it. It was another neighbor, Mrs. Miller. "They say the schoolhouse has been blown up!" she breathlessly exclaimed.

"That can't be possible," Sleight said. Again, he looked toward Kehoe's farm. In seconds, the picture had dramatically changed. Buildings on the property were now engulfed in flame. Several dull blasts sounded through the air. Sleight knew the sound immediately. It was exploding dynamite.[37]

George Hall prowled the land near his farm looking for two calves that had got loose. He saw smoke in the sky not far from his place.

Will Horning, one of Hall's neighbors, was in sight. "Did you see this smoke?" he called over.

"Yes," Horning called back. "I heard an awful explosion."

Hall got his machine and picked up Horning and another neighbor, Mrs. Virgaline Zeeb. They followed the smoke to Kehoe's farm.[38]

Monty Ellsworth was planting melons. It was a good morning for the task, quiet and sunny. Without warning, a loud noise surrounded him.[39]

Ellsworth's wife Mable was cleaning upstairs in the house when she heard a tremendous sound. Immediately she ran to a window and looked out. On a clear day she could see the chimney of the schoolhouse just a couple of miles east of the farm. Now all she could see was a cloud of white dust in the direction of Bath Consolidated.

Faint screams carried through the air.[40]

Sidney Howell was working in his yard with the help of his sons, Robb and Alden, and Melvin Armstrong, his twenty-eight-year-old neighbor. A strong report cracked through the air.

The four men looked up. "That is about the direction of the school," Howell said. Could the boiler have blown up?

A second *bang* thundered loudly. This one sounded like someone firing a high-caliber gun, and the noise was definitely closer. It seemed like it came from the Kehoe place. Smoke curled above the neighboring farm. Ready to help, the men got into Armstrong's machine and quickly drove to the scene.[41]

The Consumers Power linemen atop the wooden poles felt the ground shake. In the distance, they could see a cloud of dust. Nearby a farm was in flames. Something drastic was unfolding in Bath.

Ellsworth saw a cloud of smoke pouring out of Kehoe's barn. Clearly more than the barn was on fire. A hovering black cloud was growing over the property, thick and furious.[42]

◆ ◆ ◆

The school's roof was solidly planted on the remains of the first-floor classrooms. The outer walls had crumbled to the sides, although a back wall remained steady. It was as if a giant hand had smashed the north wing's roof into the ground, leaving the remainder of the school untouched save for the broken windows. Among the chunks of wood and broken wall, tiny bodies could be seen. The screams of children in the rubble were joined by the frantic cries of parents now flooding the grounds.

◆ ◆ ◆

Mable Ellsworth ran out of the house and joined her husband. "My God," she cried, "the school is blowed up!"[43]

Ellsworth looked east and saw a black and white plume about one hundred feet high coming from the direction of the school. Kehoe's farm would have to burn; the school children needed his help. Among the students was Ellsworth's son, a second-grade student. Ellsworth ran to his machine and headed to the scene of the disaster.

His Ford pickup was achingly slow.[44]

O. H. Buck, a Consumers Power foreman, and some of his men crawled through a broken window of the Kehoe farmhouse. They peered through the smoky living room, looking for anyone who might be caught within the inferno. For the moment the would-be rescuers holed up in the north end of the home while flames licked the southern portion.

Buck and his men called out, hoping they might reach someone trapped in the blaze. There was no answer. Instead, they decided to salvage what furniture they could before the fire spread into the living room. A davenport was shoved out the window, then a table and chairs.

Buck looked around to see what else might be saved. There was something in the corner of the room.

Dynamite.

"Without thinking much about what I was doing," Buck later said, "I picked up an armful [of the explosives] and handed [it] to one of the men."

Fig. 6. The ruins of the north wing's first- and second-floor classrooms. Note the jackets still hanging neatly on coat hooks in the upper left-hand corner. *(Courtesy of the Bath School Museum.)*

The room was thick with smoke, choking the oxygen. Buck and his men got the hell out.[45]

Hall, Horning, and Mrs. Zeeb pulled into the yard. They could see that Kehoe's barn was beyond saving, but maybe some furniture could be pulled from the house. From the looks of it, some Consumers Power men were already trying to do the same. Maybe Hall could help.

A man burst out of the house.

"My God!" he yelled. "There is enough dynamite in there to blow up the county!"[46]

Across the road Buck heard a woman's voice. "The school has been blown up!" she screamed over and over.

What was going on?

Buck and his men ran to their machines. They were needed at the school, not at this madhouse of fire and dynamite.

As they reached the car, Buck felt an enormous explosion from behind. His body slammed into a truck.[47]

As he ran across the road Hall heard explosions behind him, three, four, five, six.

Lulu Harte shouted at him, frantic. "The schoolhouse is blowed," she said.

To hell with Kehoe's place. Hall left the bizarre scene, got in his machine, and raced toward the school. He was charged with adrenaline and fear. His three children, Billy, George Jr., and Willa, were students at Bath Consolidated.[48]

◆ ◆ ◆

One look and Willett Whitney realized the school was a disaster area. He hurried from the wreck that was the north wing to the east side, hoping to find someone in charge. High school students, desperate to escape, were perched atop the roof. Superintendent Huyck came around the side of the building. In the midst of chaos, Huyck maintained his strong sense of professionalism. "Go and get some ladders," he told Whitney, "and help get those scholars off the roof."

Whitney did as he was told.[49] He ran into Arthur Woodman, who helped the older man bring a ladder back to the building.[50]

A fledgling rescue effort was under way.

Lee Mast woke up in a daze. A school desk was on top of him. He shook it off and looked up. Through the dust in the air, he could see the sky from a hole in the roof. Ahead he made out one of his classmates, Virginia Richardson, walking across the rubble. Lee stood up and took some hesitant steps. Unsure of what to do, he followed Virginia out of the school. An adult, someone who had some authority, must be told that something terrible happened.

He was joined by other children, some running, others stumbling in shock. Covered with white plaster dust, Lee and his classmates looked like ghostly apparitions wandering through the streets.[51]

Mrs. Warner ran to the back of the school. She saw, to her horror, a youngster lying still in the grass; the boy was clearly dead.[52] But sounds of life abounded with the cries coming from the rear of the building. She saw Superintendent Huyck on the roof, trying his best to make order from chaos. High school students, many ready to jump from the precarious height of the dangerous building, surrounded him. Fearing they would be injured, Huyck begged the students to hang on for a few more minutes. He spotted Mrs. Warner and called out to her. "Please," he beseeched, "bring ladders and axes."[53]

Once Frank Smith regained his bearings, he darted up a staircase, Harrington close behind him. He could see through the hallway to the south door of the school, which appeared to be relatively safe. Children from Miss Sterling's and Miss Gutekunst's rooms were lined up as though ready for a fire safety drill. Many times throughout the school year children had to practice how to evacuate in case of fire; now, with a real emergency at hand, the first- and second-grade students were putting theory into practice. Smith led them outside to safety; he noticed that Harrington was holding the door.[54]

Willis Cressman looked out the windows of the assembly hall. He couldn't see a thing through the glass, which seemed like it was enveloped in some kind of dusty cloud.

Then the cloud broke. Through the dust, Cressman saw one student jumping from the window to the ground, some twelve or fourteen feet below.

Superintendent Huyck didn't like this at all. He implored them not to jump, just please wait for someone to bring a ladder.

This was one time the students didn't care what their superintendent had to say. Windows opened, and teenagers took flight. Beneath the windows was a shack. Students jumped onto the shack's roof, quickly got their bearings, and made the second leap to the ground. It didn't seem that dangerous, and it certainly looked safer than staying in the assembly room.

Cressman made his leap, landed, and realized that the shack's roof wasn't big enough to hold everyone trying to escape. He made a second jump to the ground; it felt like he instantaneously hit the earth. Other teenagers landed all around him, thumping hard on impact. Cressman wasn't sure if they were jumping or falling. Some kids had broken legs.[55]

A little girl's body was suspended in the rubble by her heels, limp and torn like a discarded rag doll. Doris Johns, dead at age seven, hung upside down in plain view until someone got through to dislodge her body.[56]

Rubble rained down on eleven-year-old Dean Sweet. His head was badly slashed, one leg was broken, and his chest was smashed.[57]

Elsewhere in the ruins Dean's thirteen-year-old sister Ava couldn't understand why her classroom had been plunged into inky darkness. She remembered hearing a terrific roar, then being hit by things from above. Now she couldn't see a thing and couldn't move much either. A board lay atop her skull. The skin was cracked open; a map of black and blue mottled her face. Her right arm felt useless. Ava, trapped in a coffinlike space, was terrified that the layer of debris holding her in would collapse any moment and bury her.

Through the black, she could hear someone nearby, her friend Lillian Wildt. The two girls talked to one another, trying to figure out what happened and how they could get out of this trap.

There were twenty-six children in her class. All Ava knew of them now was that Lillian was alive and close.[58]

Ava and Lillian remembered an old lesson about what to do in sudden accidents: keep still. Now they took heed of the wisdom, reserving energy and oxygen should they need them later.[59]

◆ ◆ ◆

When Sidney Armstrong and the Howells pulled up to Kehoe's farm, they saw an inferno engulfing much of the property. Hot winds whipped the fire, threatening to set Armstrong's automobile ablaze. Quickly, the Howells got out so Armstrong could move his machine to safer ground.

Through the thick smoke and flame, Howell could make out a small figure next to one of the buildings. It was a man backing up a truck. The man got out of the vehicle, pulled a funnel from the gas tank, and then got back in. The truck pulled forward, disappearing into the smoke, then emerged again.

Howell could finally make out the driver. Kehoe. There was a wild gleam in his eyes, the look of someone trying to focus on a thousand visions of perdition all at once.

Before turning out onto the road, Kehoe pulled his machine up to the Howells.

"Boys," he said, "you are my friends. You better get out of here.

"You better go down to the school."

Stunned, Howell and his sons ran to the road and looked for Armstrong. Kehoe passed them, heading east.

In the direction of the school.[60]

◆ ◆ ◆

The classroom where Eva Gubbins was giving her sixth graders their geography exam was now in ruins, smashed by the falling second floor. Gubbins was in a haze, trapped by debris. A concrete beam had crushed her legs; an iron radiator was pinned against her spine. Blood seeped from gashes on her head. Gradually she became aware of her environment, her eyes adjusting to the darkened interior of the wreckage.

Just above her face, she made out the features of a schoolboy. The same beam that now pinned her in the rubble had flattened the boy's body against her legs. The child's eyes were wide open, his face just inches from hers.

She tried to move her legs, but they held fast.

The boy didn't move; he made no sound.

To her horror, Gubbins realized that the child was dead. His eyes were frozen wide open just above hers. Her screams joined other cries within the rubble. She tried to turn away, but her head was wedged tight. All Gubbins could do to avoid the boy's death stare was to close her eyes.[61]

Now on the ground, Emory Huyck picked his way through the rubble. Bodies of dead children were being pulled out; other children were digging their way out, emerging from piles of brick and wood like dust-covered moles.

Huyck gingerly picked up one boy and carried him across the bricks. The child remained unconscious as the superintendent hurried him to safety. He carried the boy to the telephone exchange office, laid him on a couch someone put on the front porch, and went back to the school.

The boy, fifth grader Carlton Hollister, it was later said, was the first injured—but alive—victim pulled from the rubble.[62]

One moment he'd been taking the sixth-grade geography exam; now Earl Proctor was wedged tight, unable to see anything. Intense pain seared up and down his lower back and into his legs. He tried to move, but the best Earl could do was wiggle his fingers a bit.[63]

Through the darkness, nine-year-old Raymond Eschtruth stared at a beam of light about the size of a dime. He called for the janitor. No answer.

Maybe I'm dreaming, Raymond thought to himself.

Gradually he realized this was no dream. Unable to move, he concentrated on what he'd done earlier that morning. He was pretty sure he'd gotten all his chores done. But how he'd gotten trapped beneath the bricks, that was a mystery. The last thing he remembered was being in Miss Weatherby's room, then all went black. He hadn't heard any noise.

Raymond felt something pressing against him from above. It was another child. He wriggled a little and finally was able to move his right arm.

How on earth had he and the other kid ended up like this? It was too much to comprehend. Mercifully, Raymond lost consciousness.[64]

Elsewhere in the rubble, Raymond's eleven-year-old sister Marian—like her brother—thought she was in the midst of some terrible dream. She hadn't heard the explosion at all. She opened her eyes, wondering if she had just woke from a deep sleep.

Piles of plaster and other debris covered her. Marian screamed. She didn't stop screaming, not for hours, hoping someone would hear her.[65]

The explosion at 8:45 drew people from their homes, customers from the barbershop and pharmacy on Main Street, businessmen, housewives, and farmers from the fields surrounding Bath. The scene was dire. It was later estimated that 230 to 275 children were in the building at the time of the blast. Just about every family in the area had at least one child at Bath Consolidated School; some had more.

The familiar faces of Bath were all at the scene. Glenn Smith—Frank's younger brother—the local postmaster who was celebrating his birthday on this day. His father-in-law, Nelson McFarren. Leonard Hiatt, who operated a Standard Oil gas station. Simeon Ewing, Bath's grocer and the chief township officer. Jay Pope and his son-in-law, Lawrence Hart. Ed Drumheller, the local highway commissioner.

Homes were opened as temporary hospitals. Bedsheets became bandages as wounded children were brought out of the wreckage. Mrs. Warner and other women made coffee and sandwiches; the men would need food to keep up their strength for the heavy work.

The school was a site of epic destruction and epic heartbreak. Parents, desperate to find their children, clawed with bare and bloodied hands through the wreckage. On the sidewalk in front of the school, one man knelt over the body of his dead son. Wracked with grief and shock, the man slammed his hands into the ground over and over, screaming prayers.[66] A mother and father, voices drained by shock, wandered the grounds, asking in a heavy German accent, "Have you seen our liddle Mary?"[67]

Parents called out names. The lucky ones had frantic reunions, pulling their dust-covered children into tight hugs.

Slowly, on a grassy field in front of the school, a morgue was growing. Blankets covered each body as dead children were laid out. Mothers and fathers, partially in hope of what they wouldn't find, but mostly in dread of what might be underneath, gingerly lifted blanket edges for a glimpse of the body. Now and then, a howling cry of anguish pierced the chaos of rescue as parents identified a dead child.

Working through her own pain, Evelyn Paul shepherded her students toward the light. She climbed over a window ledge, dropped to the ground, and commanded her girls to jump into her arms.[68] One girl, Albert Detluff's daughter Marcia, had a deep wound in her ankle.[69] Her father, guided it would seem by sheer parental instinct, arrived on the scene within moments. With help of his mother-in-law, Detluff carried his bleeding daughter to safer ground and then home where he bandaged her ankle. Once Marcia was stabilized, Detluff went back to the school to see what more he could do.[70]

Fifteen minutes had passed since the initial explosion at the school and the fire at Kehoe's. Amid the screams, debris, and mass confusion, it seemed more like an eternity compressed by chaos.

◆ ◆ ◆

Workers peeled back more of the roof. Two boys, huddled beneath the debris and clearly terrified, were released. They needed no help from the rescuers at that point, picking themselves up and running away from the field of destruction as fast as they could.

If two boys had been found alive then there might be more in that section. Gingerly the crew lifted out huge beams splintered and sagging onto piles of collapsed bricks. The work was steady but agonizingly slow

Fig. 7. The temporary morgue. *(Courtesy of the Bath School Museum.)*

as they realized the form of another child lay just beneath their hands. Their work became more heated, brick by brick by brick.

The child, a boy, was covered with dust and did not appear to be breathing.

The work continued. They reached the body, preparing to transfer the tiny corpse to the growing lawn morgue.

Suddenly the child sat up. He rubbed his eyes, looked at the workers and let out a "phew!" of relief.

Before they could get his name, the boy raced across the mountainous debris and into the crowd. [71]

Monty and Mable Ellsworth ran across the front lawn of the school, desperate to find their son. He's safe, someone told them. We've got to help the children inside.

Ellsworth looked at the rubble. Beneath the heavy roof he could see a group of five and six year olds trapped in a grisly pile. Their small body parts—heads, arms, and legs—poked out at random from the debris. A sickly cover of dust, plaster, and blood made it impossible to tell who the children were.

With no cranes or heavy equipment immediately available, work was done with the most rudimentary of tools—steady hands and strong backs. The heavy roof was a major concern. It needed to be wrenched free if the men were to reach the children trapped farther inside the north wing. Perhaps it could be moved with rope.

"I have lots of rope in my slaughterhouse," said Ellsworth. He ran back to his Ford pickup and headed for home.[72]

Detluff headed toward the telephone exchange on Main Street. Run by seventeen-year-old Lenora Babcock, the exchange was Bath's communications center. Certainly calls had to be made to inform the authorities in Lansing and ask for help from nearby communities. Within all the confusion, it was important to make sure no one forgot this task.

Babcock worked the lines furiously. She called Lansing, Dewitt, and other nearby towns. "The school has been blown up!" she repeated over and over. "We need help."[73]

Huyck—still a calm center in the maelstrom—was at the telephone exchange as well. Now that the initial rescues were under way, the superintendent had taken it upon himself to make sure calls went out for help. "Bert," Huyck told Detluff, "there is no use calling anybody. I have done all that can be done. I have called the State Department and the State Police, and there is no help that you can get. It is all done."

"All right," Detluff replied. "I will go and get a private doctor for my girl."[74]

It took only moments for Chief Hugo Delfs, head of the Lansing Fire Department, to assess the situation once he got word of the unfolding disaster. The details from Bath indicated a disaster of unprecedented dimensions. Delfs's response had to be of the highest order. He first sent out a chemical firefighting unit under the supervision of his assistant chief Paul Lefke. Next went a truck with telegraph and telephone equipment. Communications, Delfs knew, were vital.

The trucks roared toward Bath, sirens wailing. It took just twelve minutes from the time Delfs got the call for the rescue vehicles to arrive on the scene.[75]

Assistant Chief Lefke couldn't believe his eyes. He'd seen disasters before, but nothing in his professional career had prepared him for this. The school looked like a building destroyed by guns or bombs during the world war. Bodies were on the ground, the wounded, the dying, the dead—all children. Adults were running everywhere. Some carried bleeding children; some provided supplies to workers. Others knelt beside small, still bodies. The cries of these parents were ghastly, the sounds of people ripped to the core with sudden grief.

Their wails were mixed with unearthly sounds emerging from the school rubble, terrified children screaming for deliverance.[76]

The chief of security for the Fisher Body Plant, an automobile supply factory, in nearby Flint, was in Bath for the day. He heard the explosion, ran to the scene, and found a telephone. He called his superiors at Fisher, telling them, "Send every man you can to Bath."

Next he called the REO Motor Car plant in Lansing. Today the two companies weren't competitors.[77]

◆ ◆ ◆

Job Sleight at the roadside saw someone drive by in a Ford pickup. For a moment he thought it was Monty Ellsworth. Slowly he realized it was Andrew Kehoe. What on earth was he doing?

Kehoe waved and continued driving east.[78]

Homer Jennison started his morning with plans to deliver some wheat in town. He filled his cart and flicked the reins of his horses. A machine passed by. The driver looked at Jennison, nodded his head in recognition, and continued onward. The man looked familiar.[79]

Looming in the distance was a farm, its buildings ablaze. Jennison picked up the trot of his horses.

He saw Job Sleight at the side of the road. He asked about the mysterious driver.

"Wasn't that Kehoe?" Jennison called out.

Sleight replied that he thought it was.[80]

Monty Ellsworth drove south from the school, then turned west toward home. He saw Kehoe driving east into town. Kehoe raised his hand, waved at Ellsworth, and gave a strange grin. It struck Ellsworth that he could see both rows of Kehoe's teeth.[81]

One youngster, pedaling his bicycle as fast as he could to get home, passed a Ford truck heading into town. Although the child was distressed, the driver ignored him.[82]

Sleight caught a ride to town on the running board of a neighbor's automobile. A war zone greeted him. Wounded children were laid out in front of Frank Smith's house.

Someone asked Sleight to bring water. He got a pail and took water to the children on Smith's lawn.

"What's the matter with me?" asked one boy. "I can't move."

Sleight could see the boy trying to wiggle his shoulder. A fist-sized lump jutted from the child's head.

"What is on my left hand?" the child asked.

It struck Sleight that the boy's mangled hand looked like a pumice stone.[83]

One kindergartner ran wildly from the scene as fast as his legs could move. His mother met him at the door of their home, her eyes glued to the disaster unfolding at the school. Seeing her baby, coming home safe filled her with relief.

"Why are you carrying that chair?" she asked.

It was only then that the child realized he'd picked up his chair when he fled the school and carried it all the way home.[84]

Monty Ellsworth threw his ropes and a block and tackle set into the back of his Ford. He jumped back in the truck and raced to the disaster zone.

Just after ten o'clock Charles V. Lane, chief of the Fire Marshall Division of the Michigan Department of Public Safety, got word of an explosion in Bath. He headed to the scene.[85]

As he woke, Raymond Eschtruth realized someone was carrying him. The stranger brought the boy across the lawn and placed him on the sidewalk with some other children.

Raymond's mind was in a fog. He felt no pain, though he was amazed at all the dust covering his body. His eyes and ears were filled with plaster and blood.

Someone came up to him, a neighbor, and sat down. Her brother, one of Raymond's classmates, was dead, she told him.

It was all so confusing. Raymond didn't know what to think.[86]

Frank Smith's house, located across the street from the school, was one of many homes serving as a temporary triage center. Wounded children were being brought there, then loaded into automobiles for transport to hospitals in Lansing. Rows of hastily installed cots filled the living room; other wounded children were tucked into the Smiths' bed.

Superintendent Huyck, fresh from the telephone exchange, looked over the situation. With Smith's wife Leone at his side, he paused at the makeshift bedside of one little girl.

"I think she is dying," he said. Leone Smith thought so, too.

Huyck asked Mrs. Smith if she could accommodate more children. She told him yes; as she went upstairs to open more rooms for the wounded, Huyck quickly went back to the killing zone to see what else he could do.

Minutes later, as Leone came back downstairs, the house was rocked by another explosion.[87]

Flames licked the Kehoe house and barn, rapidly consuming the structures. Periodically there was a loud *bang* from inside, as though someone had randomly fired a gun.

Driving east, Chief Lane saw a farm with buildings ablaze; he drove by the inferno but didn't stop. The school disaster took precedence over a house fire.[88]

◆ ◆ ◆

Leona Weldon, a secretary in the Lansing office of the American Red Cross, wasn't a field worker, but she knew how to pull people together. She started when a staff member at the Social Service Bureau, located just across the hall, notified the Red Cross of the explosion. Thrust into a crucible, Weldon kept her cool. She started making calls. Organization of a relief effort was under way.[89]

◆ ◆ ◆

Dart Lang and John Snively, Consumers Power employees, headed toward the schoolhouse, ready to help. John Curtis, a fellow Consumers Power worker who had already been at the scene, stopped the men. "If you haven't got a strong heart," he warned Lang, "you'd better not go up."

"Somebody better go up," Lang replied.

Lang suddenly heard a car behind him. The machine was clearly going pretty fast and wasn't going to let anything get in its way.

"Hot rail!" Lang yelled to Snively. The two men dove into a nearby ditch.

The automobile, which Lang could see was a Ford pickup, drove on. "What is the matter with that man?" said Lang. "Is he crazy?"

He watched as the machine swerved to the right, in front of the wreckage of Bath Consolidated School.[90]

Jay Pope looked over the smashed school roof. Perhaps, he said to his son-in-law, Lawrence Hart, we can pry the roof up with a telephone pole. Hart agreed. He headed toward the road, where he ran into Frank Smith.

"Let's get a telephone pole," said Hart.

The two needed a car big enough to carry a pole. Hart's truck was at the grain elevator in town, too far to run for the moment. In the crowd, Hart saw Huyck's wife Ethel. The Huycks owned a four-door Ford sedan, a machine big enough to transport a telephone pole and then some.

Ethel Huyck told Hart and Smith they could use her car but her husband had the keys. Could the superintendent be found amid the confusion?

"Maybe I can start the car with my jackknife," Hart said.

He got under the dashboard and fiddled at the ignition with his knife blade. A spark lit up, kicking off the machine's engine.

Hart and Smith drove three blocks to a spot where they knew some unused telephone poles lay on the ground. With the help of men already at the scene, including Smith's brother Glenn, they managed to fit a telephone pole into the sedan.

They drove back quickly, pulling up to the school. Hart didn't want to park too close to the building. What was left of it could collapse without warning.

In his rearview mirror, Hart noticed a Ford truck directly behind him drawing up to the curb.[91]

A young garage mechanic, Elton McConnell, had been helping pull children from the debris. For some reason, he left the scene, passing a truck as it pulled up. McConnell recognized the machine as Andrew Kehoe's, a man he knew from around town.[92]

Dart Lang saw a flash and heard an explosion. It sounds like a bomb dropped from an airplane, he thought. A great cloud of smoke rose from the street. When it cleared, Kehoe's machine was gone.[93]

Within the rubble Beatrice Gibbs was in bad shape. Her left arm and both her legs were fractured. She was bruised and cut all over.

What had happened? It just didn't make sense. Why, yesterday she had turned ten years old; now she was trapped, broken and bleeding. She could see a radiator dangling just above her. The pain was too much; Beatrice finally passed out.

A sudden *boom* from somewhere nearby shook the debris. Beatrice woke up and opened her eyes. The radiator was gone.[94]

Always a professional, Chief Lane quickly assessed the frenzied situation. Other people clearly were handling the rescue; he needed to concentrate on his task at hand. He was intent on finding the cause of the explosion. A gut feeling told him that some kind of high-test gasoline had caused it. Rural schools throughout the area employed this volatile fuel—commonly used to power airplanes—to run furnaces. This practice, Lane felt, was dangerous, potentially deadly, a devastating accident waiting to happen.

Lane poked through the basement but saw no signs of a gasoline explosion. Maybe someone upstairs, perhaps another fire official on the scene, would have more information.

Debris was everywhere. Lane stepped over a chunk of what looked like rubble.

It was strangely quiet down there. Compared to the chaos outside, Lane was surrounded by relative silence.[95]

Although she didn't take any children into her home, Mrs. Warner's house was a hub of activity. People came for bedding and cots to be used in the triage area. Now Mrs. Warner was making sandwiches and coffee. It was hard to believe that just fifteen minutes had passed.

Without warning a second explosion—louder this time—sent Mrs. Warner reeling. She heard glass breaking as windows shattered. A lock blew out of one of her doors; screws skittered across the floor like mice.[96]

Don Ewing went from playing catch to rescuing children. He wondered what could have caused such a horrendous explosion. Maybe a boiler in the cellar had exploded. If not that, maybe something in the chemistry laboratory had gone horribly wrong.

He pulled a few victims from the wreckage of the school and then went looking for his mother. Suddenly Ewing heard a second explosion.

A car must have caught fire, he thought. A gas tank must have exploded.[97]

The explosions at Kehoe's farm could be heard at the school. One child, safely out of the wreckage, believed the sound was an approaching thunderstorm. We'd better run because it's going to rain, he thought.

Another boom sounded through the air. Through the treetops, the child saw a ball of flame.[98]

Lawrence Hart and Frank Smith were joined by a couple of men who helped them get the telephone pole out of Huyck's sedan. The men dragged the heavy pole toward the collapsed roof where it could be put into place as a crude lever.

Moving the pole was no easy task, but the group was determined. They had got ten or twelve feet when Hart heard another blast. This one knocked him to the ground.[99]

Age was no impediment when it came to rescuers. Martin Milliman, a spry seventy-two year old, was one of the first on the scene. He'd already pulled four bodies out of the ruins. It wasn't enough. He was determined to save as many as he could.

He was working over another youngster entombed in the debris, trying to saw a plank that held her fast.

From behind him there was a sudden explosion and the sound of screams. Inexplicably Milliman felt all his strength suddenly vaporize.[100]

From behind him, Elton McConnell heard an enormous *boom!* He turned to see an automobile blow sky high.[101]

O. H. Buck, the Consumers Power man, couldn't believe what he saw. First the burning house, now a school in shambles. He could hear the voices of children crying out from the rubble.

Just as at the house, Buck felt an explosion come from behind, and again was knocked off his feet.

He looked back over his shoulder. A terrible black cloud of smoke mushroomed over what looked like a blasted automobile.[102]

A loud report shook the air. Raymond Eschtruth and his neighbor jumped. The two boys took off, each in a different direction.

Raymond didn't realize his leg was broken. He ran hard, getting away from the explosion as fast as he could.[103]

Another child fleeing from the blast heard someone scream, "The trees are full of it!" What did that mean? Were the trees packed with dynamite?[104]

Albert Detluff, helping out in the back of the building, heard an enormous roar, the sound of what had to be a second explosion. He ran toward the noise.[105]

Josephine Cushman froze in amazed horror as metal flew through the air up into the sky.

An airplane, she thought, this was all done by an airplane. We must be under attack.[106]

George Hall pulled up and saw Huyck standing by Kehoe's machine. The two men exchanged words.

There was a flash, lighting up Hall's eyes. He couldn't believe what he'd just seen. Kehoe just disappeared like in a magic trick.[107]

◆ ◆ ◆

Accounts differ as to exactly how it happened. In the madness of the moment, logic and coherence were among the first casualties. What can be strung together from eyewitness accounts and news reports is this.

Kehoe drove up to the school and called Huyck to his machine. The superintendent hurried over, a natural reaction. Kehoe was a school board member and must be informed of the unfolding situation. It's unlikely Huyck knew that Kehoe's farm was ablaze.

When Huyck reached the truck, he asked Kehoe for help. His machine was needed to haul rope and poles for the improvised rescue.

The superintendent put his foot on the running board of the Ford.

"All right," Kehoe replied. "I'll take you with me."

Instantly Huyck was filled with horror. "You know something about this, don't you?" he blurted.[108]

Kehoe pulled out either a rifle or a pistol (some thought he flipped a switch), and fired inside the cab of his truck. Huyck may have tried to stop him. Regardless, Kehoe's shot was on the mark, hitting a cache of dynamite inside the machine.

Flaming balls of gasoline ascended through the air as the car bomb set off a new wave of destruction. The blast ripped Huyck's and Kehoe's bodies apart. Limbs were ripped from sockets; skulls burst; bodies flew high into the air.

A wide circle of hot metal shards flew outward from the Ford. It wasn't just the body of the machine ripping through the air; Kehoe had packed his truck with scraps of metal, used farm implements, nuts, bolts, and nails. The force of the explosion turned these loose items into deadly shrapnel.

The truck explosion, like the schoolhouse bomb, was heard throughout Bath and beyond. At the epicenter already frayed nerves reached the breaking point. People hit the ground. The screams of children and adults wracked the air. Automobiles near the truck bomb caught fire.

The fragmented remains of two adult male bodies slammed across the grounds. They landed far apart, about sixty feet from the scene, a good distance from Kehoe's exploded truck.

Shrapnel ripped into bodies. A bolt hit Cleo Clayton, who'd escaped from his classroom without injury. It tore into the boy's stomach and then drove farther into his body, lodging into his spine.[109]

Anna Perrone, the Italian immigrant, saw the car explode from her vantage point one block away. A burr, about two inches square, tore into her eye. Another piece of metal blew a three-cornered hole in her skull. Amazingly, Perrone's maternal instincts held fast; neither her baby, Rose, whom she held in her arms, nor her toddler, Dominic, who was at her side, were injured. It was as though Anna willed her children's safety.[110]

Steven Stivaviske, a sixth grader, lay in the street with both legs broken. A piece of metal blasted into his arm above the elbow. It stayed in his body, resting sickeningly just beneath the skin.[111]

F. M. Fritz, a father with three children at Bath Consolidated, was struck by a bolt in the chest above his heart. The metal worked its way up to his shoulder, fracturing and ricocheting off the bone, then headed down his arm, stopping just above his elbow.[112]

Fig. 8. The remains of Kehoe's truck. *(Courtesy of the Bath School Museum.)*

Perry Hart was struck in the heel by a piece of iron about two inches big. The shrapnel lodged in Hart's ankle as he fell, bleeding profusely.[113]

Thelma Medcoff, who stood about fifty feet from the blast site, was hit in the legs by flying metal. Blood poured from her legs out of three separate openings.[114]

The carnage closer to the car yielded more horrific results. Nelson McFarren was killed instantly by the blast; he lay dead under a tree where his body landed. His son-in-law, Glenn Smith, was mortally wounded. His entire left side was in ruins, one leg sheared off at the thigh, hand mangled, and body blackened.[115] Metal gouged a deep hole just above his right ankle.[116] B. D. Rice, a veterinarian who'd been examining farm animals nearby, applied his medical talents to the dying man, attaching splints to Smith's damaged right leg.[117] A Consumers Power man used a belt to stem the bleeding from the stump of the ruined left leg. Amazingly, Smith could speak. "I have been hit," he told his brother Frank, the school janitor. "It is all up with me." Over and over he whispered to his caregivers, "I don't want anybody to feel bad if I go."[118]

Someone grabbed Principal Huggett. A panicked voice declared that the explosions were all a "set job." "They got Mr. Huyck!" Huggett was told. "They will get you!"[119]

Huggett assessed the situation. Before him the school lay in ruins. Children were dead, dying, and wounded. Cars were in flames; the body of his superintendent, the bodies of his friends, lay dead in the streets. To the west, a farm was blazing.

"I realized there was nothing I could do," Huggett later said. "I went on helping the youngsters there."[120]

Chapter 8

A SCHOOL, A FARM

Ugly smells fouled the air. The fragrant aroma of morning lilacs was overpowered by the stench of dynamite, smoke, flame, gasoline fumes, blood. As the sickly fumes lingered in nostrils throughout the killing zone, the collective understanding of Bath changed. It wasn't an exploded boiler that leveled the school. Kehoe's farm was ablaze. Kehoe blew himself to bits. Kehoe was at the center of the horror.

Chunks of human flesh entangled in the wires above. Blood dripped like a red, misty rain. A ruined chassis and motor were all that remained of Kehoe's truck. A steaming tangle of intestines were lodged in the steering wheel.[1]

Carnage was strewn across the ground, and in the trees. The helter-skelter scattering of blood, limbs, bones, guts, and inner organs looked like the remnants of a slaughterhouse hit by a tornado.

Many couldn't take it. Stomachs curdled. Foul smells of raw and half-roasted meat—of human origin—were soon mixed with a horrible vomitlike stench.

Carlton Hollister had no idea where he was or how he got there, but he found himself lying on a couch on the porch of the telephone office, a block and a half from the school. Through a haze he could hear Lenore Babcock, the telephone operator. Her words sounded strange.

"The school has blown up," she was saying. "We need help."

Gradually Carlton's mind wrapped itself around Babcock's words.

"People are dead and injured," Babcock continued. "Many are trapped in the wreckage."

Now Carlton understood. There had been a disaster at the schoolhouse. Somehow he'd survived it.[2] The fifth grader had no clue that his rescuer, superintendent Huyck, was now dead.

Nellie and Albert Cushman pulled their car up to the scene, a vision of bedlam. Someone told them that Ralph had suffered a broken leg, but they quickly learned that was a different Ralph, not their son.

Josephine Cushman saw her parents, worked her way through the crowd, ran to them, and got into the car. The first words from her mother were a mixture of fear and anticipation. "Where's Ralph?" Nellie asked.

"He hasn't come out of the school yet, I know it," Josephine said.

Suddenly Josephine felt a pain just above her knee. It was only then that she realized shrapnel from the car explosion had hit her in the leg.[3]

In Pontiac, some eighty-five miles from Bath, Chester Sweet got word about the explosion. His niece and nephew, Dean and Ava, were students at the school. Nothing could stop him from getting to the scene.

He pushed his machine as hard as he could, the speedometer topping near an achingly slow forty-five miles an hour. Still, Sweet drove like hellfire, powered by gasoline and adrenaline. The car hung in mile after agonizing mile.

When he arrived, Chester immediately threw himself into the rescue effort. His timing was immaculate; when Sweet hit Bath, his machine shook and shuddered, blew out, and died.[4]

One anonymous worker had no idea where his son was. He was torn with anguish yet knew there was nothing he could do about the situation. He swallowed hard and did his duty.

The man found the body of a girl, all life gone. More thoughts of his son haunted him. He muscled on, determined to do what had to be done.

Beneath the rubble, he heard a call. "Daddy!" It was another girl, probably a foot below the surface from the way her voice sounded. She cried out again. "Daddy, come and get me."

Following the noise, the worker pulled brick after brick loose, reaching a board that held the girl within the pile. He tried to reassure her. "Yes," he told her, "your daddy will be here in a few minutes."

The board held tight. Mustering all he had, the worker pulled and strained. With a *snap* the board broke loose, freeing the youngster from entombment. Other than a few bruises, the girl was unhurt. She rushed to another man just a few feet away. He was the child's father, unaware of how close he'd been to his daughter.

The worker said nothing. He went back to his task, praying that he might find his son just as safe as this girl.

Later that afternoon he got word. His son had been hurled through a first-story window by the explosion. The boy, thankfully, was just fine.[5]

◆ ◆ ◆

Sheriff Bart Fox received news from Bath around ten o'clock. Details were scarce. There was a disaster at the school. A building had collapsed. Children killed. Help was needed.

He grabbed the county prosecutor William Searl, and the two headed to Fox's machine. It must have been a gut instinct on the sheriff's part, taking the prosecutor. Fox didn't know what he'd find in Bath. Maybe it was a mechanical failure of massive proportions, but it could be something criminal. Fox wasn't taking any chances.

His office, located in the Clinton County center of Saint Johns, was twenty miles or so from the bomb site.[6]

◆ ◆ ◆

On an embankment near the wreckage Mrs. Eugene Hart, sitting with three of her children, resembled Michelangelo's *Pieta*. Her daughters Iola and Vivian rested in death on either side of her as she cradled her son Percy—bleeding profusely, his life fading—in her arms.

Somewhere else Mrs. Hart's son Perry tried to breathe, his body wracked with an unholy pain shooting up from his ankle, so horribly ripped apart by shrapnel from Kehoe's truck.[7]

Someone found Chief Charles Lane and gave him the news; amazingly, while investigating the basement, he hadn't heard the sound of Kehoe's truck blowing up. Lane quickly got to the site where he helped move two casualties from the school entrance.[8]

Throughout the killing field, mothers and fathers held lifeless bodies close. Blood and dust intermingled into a strange sort of mud that streaked parent and child. Howls of grief and torment blistered the air.[9]

Dragging his broken leg, Raymond Eschtruth managed to get to a cousin's house near the school. The house was a mess, all the windows blown out and shards of broken glass scattered helter-skelter. Raymond's mother took her son to her mother's house. It was obvious that the child needed a doctor's care and soon.[10]

Eventually Raymond was put into a Model T Ford for what was hoped to be a fast trip to the Saint Lawrence Hospital in Lansing. Driving conditions wouldn't allow it. The roads were clogged with machines.

These autos weren't just ambulances and police cars, fire trucks, or more rescue workers. A wave of cars packed with macabre tourists was descending on Bath, curious as hell to see what was going on.

None of it mattered to Raymond. He was still in a daze, totally unaware of what had happened to him or why.[11]

◆ ◆ ◆

Personnel at the Edward W. Sparrow Hospital in Lansing were warned at about ten o'clock: stand by. Explosion. School. Children.[12]

Hearing the sirens of approaching ambulances, doctors and nurses braced themselves.

Doors banged opened; the first wave arrived. Stretchers bearing children, shrouded with dust, bandaged, and bleeding. Pieces of brick and metal protruded from wounds. Multiple bone fractures, deep lacerations, missing fingers. Shock and terror in victims' eyes.

Blanche Hart lay on a stretcher, her body fiercely mangled. A nurse, looking at the woman, thought, "She's really blown apart."

Cars followed ambulances. Adults brought in more children, arms cradling blood-soaked youngsters. Doctors looked over the wounded, and made snap decisions. Called out who needed care first, ordered pain shots with a shout of "Hypo!" (for hypodermic needle), barked "Help him here" or "This one goes to emergency." Wheelchairs and stretchers bearing the wounded filling the corridors, nurses offering comfort—such that they could—to frightened children.

Some of the doctors, veteran medics who had served in the Great War, hadn't seen such carnage since working in makeshift battlefield hospitals.

Another wave of humanity arrived: frantic parents desperate to find this son or that daughter.

Outside the emergency room, a strange ambience enveloped the hospital. No one knew what to say. Words could not make sense of the chaos. Heavy silence stalked the hallways, offices, waiting rooms.

Beds were hastily installed in the hallways of the hospital's second floor. Sparrow lacked a pediatric ward; this corridor would have to do for the moment.[13]

◆ ◆ ◆

When Dean Sweet was found, he clearly was dead. No pulse. His crushed and broken body resembled an old rag doll torn and discarded beneath the wood, brick, plaster, and dust. A nearby wall was close to collapsing, threatening to bury the child further.

Dean's body was removed with great care, then transported to the temporary morgue on the lawn.[14]

The digging contained scenes of horrific near misses and gruesome failures. William Klock, a deputy sheriff, found a youngster lying on the rubble. Before he could lift the unconscious child to safety, a precarious brick wall collapsed. The boy was crushed, Klock's rescue thwarted by seconds.

Still the lawman pressed on. He came upon the legs of a little girl sticking out of the pile, her torso buried beneath. Klock steadied himself, and assessed the situation.

He took hold of the girl's foot; it snapped off in Klock's hands.[15]

As hard as he tried, Martin Milliman, the seventy-two-year-old volunteer, just couldn't work his saw. He was desperate to help, but the sight of Glenn Smith's wife cradling her husband's mangled body just tore him up.

Another worker told the elderly man to leave. Struggling internally with what was unfolding in his beloved town, Milliman found his way out of the pile, through the maddened crowds, and home.[16]

One rescuer saw something, maybe a stick, lying on the ground. But the stick was an unusual shape and color, definitely something out of the ordinary. He reached over to pick it up.

The stick turned out to be a human backbone.[17]

Rescuers from around the area responded to the spreading news. Dr. Milton Shaw, head of the Red Cross team, was the first medical official to arrive. He was followed by an army of doctors and nurses from Lansing's Sparrow and Saint Lawrence hospitals. There were medical workers from nearby towns and hamlets. Triage units sprouted across the lawns. Patients were prepped for ambulances.

Other rescuers poured in from throughout central Michigan. Professional and volunteer firefighters. Workers from automobile plants. Students from Michigan State College. Farmers. Factory and construction workers. Anyone and everyone within earshot of the blast.

Utter horror was countered by a ragtag collection of make-do saints.

When the school exploded Clare Gates was thrown headfirst through a window. He got up and ran for half a mile before he turned around to see what had happened. Hearing screams from the rubble, Gates ran back to the school.

He joined Howard Cushman, who'd been standing outside the school when he was knocked over by the first explosion. Gates and Cushman, both sixteen, paired up in the rescue effort. One, two, three, four, they dug out child after child.

All the kids they found were hurt to varying degrees. One small boy— a kid both Gates and Cushman knew well—was missing a leg.[18]

When George Carpenter, a new member of the Michigan State Police, heard the report of an explosion in Bath, he took to his Harley motorcycle, revved the engine, and headed out.

On the horizon as he approached the town was a strange cloud of dust. Screams filtered down the road.

He pulled up to the school. He could see the collapsed roof, a death trap for children covered in blood-muddied dust. Carpenter was grabbed by another officer.

They lifted a beam that blocked their way to the center of the rubble.

Fig. 9. Nurses preparing wounded for transportation to the hospital.
(Courtesy of the Bath School Museum.)

Carpenter and his newfound partner then worked their way across an unsteady path of brick, wood, and plaster.

They could see a woman in bricks up to her waist, her upper body poking from the rubble like a precious flower.

Two children—both dead—were nestled in her arms. Carpenter and his partner gently lifted their bodies from the woman's protective grasp as she feebly let go.

The woman, Hazel Weatherby, somehow had managed to keep the children close to her from the moment the roof caved in. Once the officers had her students, Weatherby gave in to death.[19]

◆ ◆ ◆

Sheriff Fox and William Searl knew they were nearing Bath when they saw the cars. Machines were backed up on the main road into town.

Fox drove his official automobile around the traffic jam. He was waved through cordons set up by State Police officers on the scene. He

Fig. 10. Loading an ambulance in the shadow of destruction. *(Courtesy of the Bath School Museum.)*

and Searl passed through the barrier, soaking in the incredible scene. It was monumental destruction beyond their comprehension.

People running: men, women, teenagers, children. Howls of anguish, cries for help, sounds of automobiles, the clunky bang of bricks falling or being tossed. The north wing of the school building now a mound of rubble pockmarked with frantic men pulling at debris. White sheets, stained with blood, covering what must be small bodies stretching across the lawn. The smoking remains of some sort of vehicle. A few cars nearby, ruined by fire.

A vision of hell on earth.

Fox and Searl got out of the car. The area was, for all practical purposes, the scene of a crime. Kehoe's name was being whispered as the man behind it all. Kehoe's farm was burning. Kehoe blew himself up and took Superintendent Huyck with him.

The sheriff didn't have much time to look; someone quickly asked him to come to a nearby ditch.[20]

Across from the school, on the edge of Frank and Leone Smith's property, a pair of volunteers from Lansing, Alex Urqhart and Dr. Milton Shaw, the Red Cross director, were making bandages for victims. One of them noticed something at the side of the road, a reddish lump with tattered clothing. They went over to investigate.

Urqhart, a veteran of the world war, was unnerved. He'd seen a lot of carnage in his day, sights that would turn a man's blood cold, things that could shock a soul to its core. Yet nothing he'd seen in the Great War could compare to what lay in the ditch.

It was a body, albeit one blown all to hell. The corpse was completely gutted, a ripped up carcass, a hunk of meat and bone. Though the body was in shambles, the face and head were more or less intact. Grey hair matted what remained of the skull.

Gingerly they walked to the clump. In the mess of clothes, two documents poked out of a fold that once might have been a coat or shirt pocket.

One item was a driver's license, the other a bankbook. Both were issued in the name of Andrew P. Kehoe.

A woman, hair wild, face streaked with dirty tears, stopped suddenly near the two men. Either she was running to the school or away from it; it was hard to tell.

She looked at them. "What's the name?" she said.

Urqhart examined the papers.

"Andrew Kehoe."

"That's the man!" the anonymous woman screamed.

Up in the telephone wires, they could see part of an automobile, the headlight attached and glass still intact.[21]

Sheriff Fox arrived. He was handed the license and bankbook. The lawman carefully studied the documents.

Still, no assumptions were made that these human remains were Kehoe's. A positive identification had to be made. And there was enough left of the face on this mess to complete the task.

A high school boy who had a passing acquaintance with Kehoe was brought to the scene. The kid was pretty sure this was the man. Mel Kyes, who sat on the school board with Kehoe, was also brought in to look over

Fig. 11. The remains of Andrew P. Kehoe. *(Courtesy of the Bath School Museum.)*

the face. The lifeless countenance, as near as Kyes could tell, was indeed Kehoe's.

Finally they fetched Sydney Howell, Kehoe's neighbor, who was always friendly with the man. Howell, more than anyone, could positively identify the remains.

Howell clambered into the ditch, shaky over what he might see. He took in the gruesome sight. Eyes, nose, face, hair: yes, the clump was Kehoe.

Terrible feelings gripped Howell to the core. How could this man, his neighbor, burn down his farm, blow up a school, kill so many children, then blast himself and Huyck to pieces? It wasn't the Andrew Kehoe he knew.

In the days to come, Howell struggled with these thoughts.[22]

A member of the Michigan State Police handed Chief Lane the damning evidence found at the Kehoe place. "I want to place this in your charge," the uniformed officer told him. "It was taken from a dresser drawer at the farm."

He handed Lane four loose sticks of dynamite. No blasting caps were attached. The chief recognized this explosive as Hercules 40 percent, a common form of dynamite used in road construction or by farmers in removing old tree stumps.

High-test gasoline as a possible cause of the school explosion was no longer under consideration.[23]

◆ ◆ ◆

Gertie Burnett felt the bricks pressing down on her body. From below, she could feel someone thumping her back, over and over, maybe using trapped legs to kick out of the rubble. It was too much for one child to handle.

Stop kicking, she implored the person beneath her.

Eventually the thumping stopped.

Gertie never knew who was beneath her. When the kicking ended, she thought, that person is dead.[24]

Desperate mothers combed the killing zone, pulling at the rubble, tugging heavy wooden beams, trying to lift chunks of concrete and plaster, frantically searching for their children.[25]

◆ ◆ ◆

In the midst of the chaos, one man snuck through the crowd to the smoking remains of Kehoe's truck. He reached into the ruined cab, clipped himself a piece of intestine dripping off the steering column, and put his precious souvenir in a jar. The unknown ghoul disappeared as quickly as he arrived, artifact in hand.[26]

◆ ◆ ◆

Albert Detluff stood over a bloody mass, a terrible hunk of blood and bone and hair bearing some likeness to a human body.

The remains wore a shredded but still recognizable checkered coat. Detluff knew at once he'd found what was left of Superintendent Emory E. Huyck's body.[27]

◆ ◆ ◆

Within an opening in the rubble, some fourteen feet below, was an opening that resembled the mouth of a cave. Within it were children, trapped and unable to climb out.

Mr. Fiora, one of the schoolteachers, didn't hesitate. He jumped into the cave, dug his way through, soothed the crying children as he freed them, and handed them up to the outstretched arms of rescuers just within reach.

Fiora's search went deeper into the cave.[28]

♦ ♦ ♦

Assistant Chief Lieutenant Lyle W. Morse, one of the top men in Michigan's Secret Service Division, arrived with his assistant, Detective William Watkins, at 10:20 a.m. (Despite the same name, this Secret Service was not affiliated with the federal agency; rather, it was a bureau within Michigan's Department of Public Safety.) Like many others, Morse's original hunch after receiving word of the disaster was that the cause of the catastrophe was an exploded boiler. When he and Watkins got to the scene word was rife: Kehoe had blown himself up. Morse quickly realized that this was no mechanical accident. He went looking for the school janitor. When Morse got to Frank Smith's house, Leone Smith told him about Kehoe's remains, bankbook, and driver's license. The documents, she said, were now safe with Sheriff Fox.

D. B. Huffman approached Morse and identified himself as the express agent who had taken care of Kehoe's package earlier that morning. He asked Morse if he had any idea as to who had dynamited Bath Consolidated.

Although nothing was official ("At that time we didn't know dynamite was used," he later told the inquest),[29] Morse said that Andrew Kehoe evidently was behind the explosion. Huffman detailed his encounter with Kehoe and the box sent to Clyde Smith, the school's insurance man. Lane, who also was at the Smith home, said he'd get in touch with the intended recipient of Kehoe's package.[30]

♦ ♦ ♦

From the grassy knoll where dead children still lay in cold repose, the temporary morgue grew larger. Sheets covered the dust-and-blood-encrusted bodies silently across the grass. From beneath the shrouds, feet poked here and there. All that could be seen were the soles of shoes, some worn paper thin. Other shoes sagged, too big for the feet they covered. It was clear that some of the children went to school in hand-me-down footwear.[31]

Nellie Cushman, desperate to find Ralph, peered under the sheets. Body after body. Her boy was not there.[32]

Other parents nervously peeked beneath the bloodied sheets of the temporary morgue, looking through the corpses, praying they would not find what they were looking for. One father, weary from rescue work, looked over the rows of lifeless bodies and saw his son. "Well," he said, "there's Billy."

There was nothing he could do for Billy now. With resignation, the man returned to the killing field, hoping to find someone else's child alive.[33]

A mother searching for her son lifted a sheet. It was not a boy but a girl covered by the shroud. Sunshine, breaking through the dust in the air, spread across the child's face. Her eyes fluttered against the light.

Josephine England was badly injured but not dead.[34]

Another voice rang out, loud and clear.

"Dean's not dead! He's alive!"

It was true. A neighbor, looking sorrowfully at the body of Dean Sweet, suddenly realized that the boy was wiggling his toes.

No ambulances were available to transport Dean to Lansing. He was taken to the hospital in the only machine around: a hearse.[35]

◆　◆　◆

Loose debris tumbled down from the ceiling in the school basement. It caught the attention of Captain John O'Brien, a Lansing police officer, and William Klock, a sheriff's deputy from nearby Ingham County. The two men cautiously approached the coal room, where they could see part of the ceiling now fallen and scattered on the floor.

There was something on the floor hidden under plaster; this was the chunk of debris Chief Lane had stepped over just minutes before.

The plaster was removed, revealing dynamite connected to some kind of wire. O'Brien and Klock didn't need to search any farther. They hightailed it out of the school.[36]

At 10:45 a painful but levelheaded decision came down: stop all rescue efforts. Dynamite was beneath the school, still wired and to God knows what. Perhaps a timing device was ticking away, ready to go off at any moment. The risk was simply too great to chance more death.

Morse, Lefke, state troopers Ernest "Buck" Haldeman and Donald McNaughton, and F. I. Phippeny, a Michigan State College engineer, carefully reentered the basement, now a hot zone where anything could happen.[37] The wire was traced to a tin pipe. The pipe, connected by small bolts, ran a considerable length through the ceiling into other rooms within the basement. The team could see that this conduit was packed solid with dynamite.

More dynamite was planted in the ceiling, hidden by wire mesh covered with plaster. Wire connected the explosive caches to a blasting cap. The men followed the trail as it led them from the collapsed north wing south toward the rest of the school basement beneath the main building. More wires were found, firmly stapled to wooden beams. The staples were a bit rusty, indicating that they had been in place for some time. These wires led to more blasting caps attached to more explosives, some dynamite, other heavy sacks filled with army surplus pyrotol.

The wire trail led to a hotshot battery connected to a clock. A similar device was discovered elsewhere in the catacombs. Whoever planted these explosives clearly knew how to do it right. Had the other timers gone off and electric currents run as intended, all of Bath Consolidated School would now be rubble with every student conceivably dead or severely injured.[38]

By some miracle—be it a short in the wiring, a bad connection, or some other cause—only the north wing's explosives had detonated. Some experts suggested that Kehoe, despite all his electrical knowledge, had made a serious error. There simply wasn't enough power in the two remaining timing devices to set off the massive amount of explosives he'd planted under the main school building.[39]

Removal of these newfound explosives was critical. Haldeman and McNaughton, working in the dark basement lit only by flashlights, carefully disconnected the blasting caps from the labyrinthine wiring. They approached the delicate task with the touch of fine silversmiths; any slight mistake conceivably could result in more explosions. After this stage was safely completed, the blasting caps, wiring, dynamite, and pyrotol were removed from the building.[40]

But some cavities and burrows were too small to accommodate a full-grown man to get at the explosives. A search went out for a person pos-

Fig. 12. Michigan State Police officers holding some of the dynamite planted by Kehoe. *(Courtesy of the Bath School Museum.)*

sessed of both the size and the maturity needed to take on this dangerous job. They found their man in fourteen-year-old Chester Sweet, the older brother of Ava and Dean. No longer enrolled at Bath Consolidated, Chester had opted out of school to work on the family farm. Without hesitation, he volunteered for the potentially deadly mission. Chester was short, young, and perhaps touched with a bit of daring-do worthy of screen idol Douglas Fairbanks. Between his stature and his tenacity, State Police officials knew that Chester had the stuff they needed.

He was led into the dark passageways of the basement. Showing no fear, Chester squeezed his body through tight spaces, gently removed the dangerous material from hidden alcoves, and handed it to men waiting just beyond the entrances.[41]

More explosives were found in a carefully concealed hideaway. A trail of eaves troughs, the rain gutters found along rooftops, was precisely secreted within the basement ceiling. Rows of dynamite sticks and pyrotol lined the troughs, which were shoved deep within the recesses using either metal well rods or bamboo poles that stretched for twenty-five to thirty feet at some points.

School janitor Frank Smith spent a good deal of time beneath the school, yet never once saw the gutters. And why not? They were hidden in the ceiling, practically invisible in the darkness. Realistically, they were unnoticeable to anyone except the man who put them in place.[42]

In all, 504 pounds of unexploded dynamite and pyrotol were pulled from the building on May 18. The material included at least nine bushel baskets full of dynamite, several thirty-pound sacks of pyrotol, ten blasting caps, and two timing devices.[43] An estimated 100 pounds of explosives had detonated beneath the north wing.[44]

◆ ◆ ◆

It was supposed to be a typical luncheon, a dry, dull talk about fund-raising for Lansing's Edward W. Sparrow Hospital. Walter Foster, president of the hospital's board of directors, regarded his lunchtime crowd at the downtown Olds Hotel. Two tables reserved for doctors were empty. These guests were either headed to Bath or furiously working in the hospital's emergency room.

One of Sparrow's leading medicos, Dr. Fred Drolett, came to the luncheon, late and urgent. After the first emergency call came in from Bath, he reported, thirty-five nurses from the Sparrow and Saint Lawrence hospitals were sent to the scene bearing blankets, sheets, stretchers, and medicine. Both hospitals were given dire instructions: prepare to receive between twenty-five and thirty victims.

"This is the worst disaster I ever saw in my life," Drolett said. "While Lansing can be proud of the police, fire and hospital aid rushed to the sufferers, the catastrophe brings home the needs which this campaign is designed to care for more than anything that could have possibly happened."

Perhaps it was a little off-putting, discussing fund-raising with diners eager to hear news about the situation in Bath, but Drollet certainly knew the importance of donations. If anything, the bloody school site drove home the hospital's overall financial needs with sobering reality.

The next speaker was Fr. John O'Rafferty, a Catholic priest. He too spoke of the importance of fund-raising, telling the gathering that the spirit of God would be in anyone who donated to the hospital. The unfolding disaster only underscored this point, he said, adding that such charitable work built the character of a community.

In about forty-eight hours, Father O'Rafferty would discover for himself exactly how the disaster would affect his own character.[45]

Joseph Dunnebacke was at the luncheon, just as shocked by the sudden news as anyone else in the room.[46]

◆ ◆ ◆

In the darkness Eva Gubbins prayed for the child above her. She was alone, scared, wondering what was going on.

There was a noise like the sound of someone moving. It was close, very close.

She could see through the rubble a space next to her. A man was crawling through. Gubbins quickly recognized her would-be savior, one of her colleagues at the school, Mr. Fiora.

"Eva," he told her, "I can't get you out—we can pray."

The beam pinning Gubbins in the wreckage had to be removed before she and the dead student could be freed. The men quickly assessed the situation. Unless they supported the fallen beam, Gubbins would remain trapped.

A makeshift frame was erected. Once the beam held firm, work began. Using sledgehammers, the men struck blow after blow. Slowly, surely, the thick wood splintered. Pieces fell away, were taken out, and the hammering began anew.

When enough of the beam had been broken up, work began on the concrete chamber holding Gubbins and the boy. Minute after minute went by, an excruciatingly slow pace. Sweat rolled off the men; they refused to let up from their muscle-weary work.

It took forty-five minutes for Gubbins and her dead companion to be released.[47]

Ethel Huyck lumbered through the grounds, stunned, numbed. A pretty red-haired woman, she now was a shadow of herself, deep in shock over the devastation of the school, the enormous loss of life, and her husband's sudden, violent death.

A woman was nearby, trying to comprehend her own bitter news.

"My husband is dead," Mrs. Huyck told the woman.

The woman, Florence Hart, had just been told about her son. "My Robert is dead," she answered.

The two parted ways. There was nothing left to say.[48]

◆ ◆ ◆

An old woodshed behind Lenore Babcock's telephone office turned into a makeshift headquarters for the newspaper writers descending on Bath. An electric telegraph line was set up with wires strung to the building so reporters could flash news back to their editors.[49] Another pressroom was improvised in the train depot, now empty. The station agent was gone, looking for his son.[50]

The unfolding story sprinted across the telegraph lines. Publishers and newsreel producers in their editorial offices recognized the school bombing demanded the fastest technology available to provide details to fact-hungry newspaper readers and moviegoers.

On the edge of his family's farm, Harold Burnett later remembered, he was amazed to see a genuine airplane landing in the fields. He'd seen planes before during air shows but never one this close. It seemed as if Bath was suddenly the center of the world with farm fields transformed into landing strips.[51]

Airplanes played a significant role in getting the news out to the world in those first hours. "Representatives from newspapers in all of the large cities in the central part of the United States were at Bath Wednesday evening and Thursday forenoon obtaining photographs and news matter, much of which was rushed to their respective office by plane," wrote an anonymous reporter in the *Lansing State Journal*.[52]

They came earlier than Wednesday evening. At 12:30 p.m. Central Time (1:30 in Bath), word first reached the *Chicago Herald-Examiner*. Its editors wanted the tale told in pictures as well as words. Quickly an agent was contacted in Detroit. A secretary, in turn, found Billy Brock, a veteran flying ace of the World War and now a barnstorming stunt pilot. Brock was hired on the spot, and at 3:15 p.m. he was sent from Detroit to Lansing. In just half an hour he reached his destination, where local reporters gave Brock negative plates with some of the first photographs of the bombing. He jumped back in the plane, took to the skies, flew pell-mell to Chicago, and landed at an airport in suburban Mayfield just an hour later. Men from the paper who met Brock at the airport rushed back to the city, put the precious photographic plates in their editor's hands, and by that evening Chicagoans could see what the Bath Consolidated School looked like for themselves. The devastation, captured in bold black and white, took just a little over eight hours to move from Bath to Chicago. This rapid delivery was gleefully detailed under the headline "Blast Photos Rushed by Air for *Herald-Examiner* 'Scoop.'" No doubt the publisher enjoyed taking a jab at his slower rivals in Chicago's hypercompetitive newspaper trade.[53]

Brock wasn't the only pilot winging his way to Bath. Newsreel photographers rushed in, some shooting their stories from the ground, others from the sky. At one point a lone plane could be seen soaring just above the ruins of the school. Once word of the disaster hit the East Coast, Pathé News, the international leader in newsreel production, sent its top New York cameraman, Thomas Hogan, to shoot footage. Hogan arrived late Wednesday and filmed the devastated school well into the early morning hours of May 19. Once the job was completed, he hired a taxi and rushed along back roads to Lansing's Capital City airport. Just before 6:00 a.m. Hogan's hired plane took off for Chicago. Carl Clifford, a top pilot, made it to the Windy City just in time to meet an air mail plane heading to New York. That night filmgoers in New York and Chicago saw the first motion pictures of the Bath Consolidated School ruins, not quite thirty-six hours after Kehoe's bomb went off.[54]

Another newspaper, the *Toledo Blade* hired an airplane piloted by Leroy Davis to whisk Norman Hauger, their head photographer, to Bath. Other *Blade* staff cameramen piled into a car and hit the gas in a 130-mile race from their Ohio base to the Michigan location.

Somewhere near Jackson, Michigan, one of the engines on Davis's plane gave out. The aircraft careened wildly, then hit the ground in a hard bounce of a landing. Although pilot and passenger weren't hurt, Hauger's deadline loomed large. Gripping his cameras and film, which fortunately survived the crash, Hauger ran across the field to a nearby road. He waved his arms wildly, finally catching the attention of a passing motorist, who drove Hauger into Jackson. With little time to waste, Hauger procured a taxi to drive him to Bath, about fifty miles away. As soon as he hit town, he went into action, then got to a railway station for the trip back to Toledo.

The *Blade* photographers who drove to Bath and back had an uneventful journey, but they didn't move as quickly as Hauger. He returned Wednesday evening and prepared photographs for the morning edition; his colleagues didn't get to the office until well after midnight.[55]

◆ ◆ ◆

Although county prosecutor William Searl was well grounded in standard criminal procedures, devastation by bombing was beyond his realm of understanding.

The area was crawling with authorities: State Police, regional law enforcement officers and fire department men, National Guard and military people. Volunteers flooded the scene, breaking down the tasks at hand: search and rescue, care for the wounded, accounting for the dead. Yet at the heart of the matter a school wired to explode—and the blazing house west of town—clearly were criminal investigations under Searl's jurisdiction.

Time and again he was told that Andrew Kehoe was responsible. Searl knew the name; Kehoe had been his father's client in the recent mortgage dispute. Although he maintained an exterior cool, Searl needed some assurance. He worked his way through the sea of people in search of a telephone to call his father.

Kelly Searl couldn't believe what his son told him. A school blown up. Children dead. A spectacular murder-suicide. Preliminary reports that Andrew Kehoe—whose farm was ablaze—was behind all this mayhem.

Their conversation was brief but supportive. Kelly Searl didn't give William advice as much as the courage to face the maelstrom. Action was needed, fast, decisive action.

Searl returned to the school with no plans in mind but determination in his heart. He met with Fox, Lane, and Morse and learned what he could. He moved the morgue from the lawn to the Community Hall. A central area was needed in which to identify the dead, a place that wouldn't be in the way of rescue workers. The Community Hall, just a block from the school, was the ideal place. Bodies could quickly be transported to the location. What's more, parents could find their children in a place that provided some privacy—albeit limited—giving them some solitude for their grief. Bodies already claimed were moved from the grassy knoll into hearses; unidentified victims were taken to the Community Hall.

Next Searl demanded an inquest. Getting the facts was paramount. That process would begin the next day, he declared. Potential jurors were immediately rounded up from among the rescuers and bystanders.[56]

◆ ◆ ◆

Rescue workers stumbled over a section of debris. They'd pulled plenty of bodies, some alive, some dead, from the rubble and wanted to be sure they had found all victims before moving on.

"I think that's everyone in this area," said one of the men.

For a second silence hung in the air, then screams pierced the rubble.

Ava Sweet and Lillian Wildt heard the worker. Now, terrified that they would be left to die, the two girls released all the energy they had saved by lying still.

Their screams were answered with furious digging. When the workers reached Ava, they found her head trapped beneath a board. Unable to loosen it without the threat of hurting Ava, they sawed the board on either side of the girl's head until she could be removed safely.[57]

◆ ◆ ◆

As he left the luncheon at the Olds Hotel, someone provided Joseph Dunnebacke with a fresh copy of the *Lansing State Journal*, an "extra" edition with new details on the unfolding tragedy. A name jumped out at him: Andrew Kehoe.

It couldn't be. Though troubled by this development, Dunnebacke kept his cool. His next stop was the Saint Lawrence Hospital, where he met with the sister superior. It occurred to the attorney that she might need nurses from a hospital in nearby Jackson; Dunnebacke offered his services as a driver. No, the sister told him, they had everything under control.

Kehoe's potential involvement weighed heavy on Dunnebacke's mind. He knew what a troublesome individual Andrew Kehoe could be, but something of this magnitude? It didn't seem possible.

Dunnebacke opened the door to his law office. Three people were inside waiting: Elizabeth, Genevieve, and Loretta Price. Nellie's sisters.

Frantic and terrified, they asked Dunnebacke for help in finding Nellie. Should they try to find her in Bath, contact the Vosts in Jackson, or sit tight and hope for the best while expecting the worst?

Hoping to ease their worries, Dunnebacke drove the Price sisters to the Vost home. On their arrival, their fears amplified.

No, the Vosts told their unexpected visitors, Nellie was not staying with them. Whatever Kehoe had said over the telephone was wrong; neither Andrew nor Nellie had come calling on Monday night.

There was only one choice now. Dunnebacke and the Prices headed to Bath. Like the rescuers and emergency medical workers, the four became snarled in traffic as they approached the small town. After arriving, they talked to the Kehoes' neighbors. What about Nellie, they asked.

No one had seen her since Kehoe brought her home Monday night. All they could do now was pray.[58]

◆ ◆ ◆

Nellie Cushman waited with Josephine while Albert worked with other rescuers to find Ralph. Mother and daughter walked back and forth, waiting for any word, quiet, nervous.

There was something on the grass. Nellie thought it was something a dog might have left behind while playing.

Josephine saw the object more clearly. "No, Mom," she said. "That's a hand."

Nellie was silent.[59]

He was heavily built, this rescuer, and tearing down broken walls was a strenuous, though not difficult, task. A hearty pull on a rope and bricks fell at his feet. He continued his work. Cocooned inside the wall were the corpses of two small boys.

He could not stop. Muscles heaving, like a mighty ox pulling a plow, the man put his weight into the work, bringing down crumpled wall after crumpled wall.

One stubborn section refused to budge. The man steadied himself, threw all of his being into the task, and finally the solid bricks gave way.

The fallen stone curtain revealed another boy, broken to pieces.[60]

Lloyd Curtis, a nineteen-year-old Lansing resident, was one of many volunteer ambulance drivers. For the better part of a day and a half he did what he had to, transporting some victims to hospitals, others to funeral homes.

He also helped pick up debris, bricks, wood, and parts of bodies torn from children's frames. Pieces of skulls, fingers, legs, feet, and hands were tossed like rocks into five-gallon pails.

The grisly work stuck with Curtis for the rest of his life.[61]

Governor Fred W. Green and his wife arrived shortly after one o'clock to survey the damage. It was an overwhelming sight to Green, who had been in office for just a few months. The devastation was beyond understanding, yet a leader couldn't just wax eloquent and move on. He promised that there would be state aid in the coming days and weeks.

For now, though, more immediate help was needed. The governor rolled up his sleeves, climbed onto the rubble, and helped the rescuers remove bricks.[62]

Paul Lefke's chemical trucks were dry after pumping two sixty-gallon tanks onto the second floor of the Kehoe farmhouse. Firefighters were told that this was where Nellie Kehoe normally slept; once the blaze was quelled they hoped to find her remains.

There was nothing to do but let the Kehoe farm burn. Efforts to quell the blaze were limited at best; there also was the danger of hidden dynamite in the farm buildings.

Periodically a crash—the sound of collapsing walls, a falling roof, bursting windows—echoed across the farmland.

When the inferno died down, entrance was still impossible. Embers, intensely hot and too dangerous to traverse, glowed for hours. They shimmered with a sinister red light seemingly stoked by hellfire.[63]

Come late afternoon there was still no word about Ralph. Nellie Cushman paced the sidewalk, unsuccessfully trying to make time move faster. Despite the warm spring day, Nellie felt a chill throughout her body. "I'm cold," she said to Josephine. A woman who overheard Nellie offered the coat she was wearing.

Though grateful, Nellie was a little hesitant. "But maybe I can't find you on the grounds again to give it back," she told the woman.

"I'll find you, I'm sure," replied Nellie's benefactor. "If I don't, take the coat and go home. It's all right."[64]

C. E. Lamb, a local farmer who doubled as the county coroner, was drowning with work. Bodies at the Community Hall morgue were still unidentified. William Searl and Sheriff Fox helped Lamb with the gruesome job of identifying the corpses. Mattie Smith, another school official, painstakingly checked the school census in her hands, trying to account for every known child at Bath Consolidated. Her task took considerable time, patience, and withheld emotions. She had a job to complete; tears would come at a more appropriate time.[65]

Josephine and her mother continued their anxious sidewalk vigil. It was about four o'clock, an agonizingly long day.

A person came up to the pair. "You're wanted at the Community Hall," he said.[66]

Cleo Clayton, the second grader ripped open by shrapnel, suffered throughout the afternoon. He remained agonizingly conscious from the time he was hit until his death some seven hours later.[67]

After Station Agent Huffman informed the authorities about Kehoe's package, an intensive search began. Clyde Smith, the insurance agent to whom Kehoe sent the box, was notified. He said the package had not arrived and swore he had done nothing to anger Kehoe.

With deadly proof that Kehoe knew how to wire a bomb, finding that box was paramount. It could be set to go off at any time; just where and when that might happen added gravitas to the situation.

The afternoon came and went, and still the box was unaccounted for.[68]

Nellie and Josephine met Albert Cushman at the Community Hall.

Inside it looked like an abattoir. Blood everywhere. Puddles on the floor. Stains on dresses of the women helping to lay out bodies on chairs normally used during social events. Blood seeping through the sheets covering the dead.

The Cushman family was brought to Ralph's body. He looked as though his head had exploded. The chin was gone. Metal slivers pricked his skin. Ralph's body was broken, every bone it seemed.

Josephine suddenly felt a horrific jolt in her back, a pain shooting through her muscles, gripping her spine. It was excruciating, unlike anything she had ever felt.

She said nothing about it to her parents. They had enough on their minds.

When rescuers had found Ralph Cushman, the family was later told, he was still sitting at his desk with a classmate seated next to him. The two boys died together.[69]

◆ ◆ ◆

The destruction of Kehoe's farm was nearly perfect. House, tractor, farm equipment, all were destroyed by a combination of fire and explosives. An elaborate wiring system snaked throughout the farm grounds, sophisticated work that showcased Kehoe's expertise as an electrician. Only the chicken coop remained standing.

An unexploded bomb inside the henhouse ironically demonstrated Kehoe's talents for mechanical invention. The device resembled standard fountains used to provide drinking water to chickens. It was centered by an upside-down quart bottle filled with gasoline and tucked into a tin can. An automobile spark plug and coil intended as an ignition device were connected to the bottle, from which emanated a yarn wick. To ensure that the fire would spread, Kehoe had packed his contraption with a heavy jacket of straw. Somewhere along the line his careful wiring from the timer inside the house had failed, just like the botched timers beneath the schoolhouse.[70]

Shade trees in a small grove near the house had been cut around their bases, a practice known as girdling. Girdling is generally used to control overgrowth of trees; in Kehoe's case it was clearly an act of destruction. In another area of the property, authorities found grapevines cut off but carefully put back in place so as to appear untouched.

Within the ruins of the barn was a different kind of destruction. Kehoe's two horses—including the blind-eyed horse he'd offered to McMullen—were burned through to their skeletons. Their feet were bound with wires, effectively preventing the animals from escaping.[71]

At the edge of the farm, searchers found a plain wooden sign attached to a fence, Kehoe's last angry words stenciled on the placard for all to see.

CRIMINALS ARE MADE, NOT BORN

◆ ◆ ◆

Bath was midway along the rail line between Lansing and Laingsburg, a town about nine and a half miles from the disaster. As evening approached, a cursory check was made of packages delivered but not yet picked up from the station.

The stationmaster saw a box addressed to Clyde Smith, the Lansing insurance agent, with a return address "Andrew P. Kehoe." Apparently the Lansing destination had been misread as Laingsburg, and thus the package hadn't been delivered to the intended recipient.

The wooden box had other words on it, markings from the crate's original contents. They loomed large.

"High Explosives. Dangerous."

Morse and another Michigan Secret Service member, Detective William Watkins, headed to Laingsburg where they took charge of the package. They handled it as gently as fine crystal from the moment it was picked up, put in the truck, and finally unloaded in Lansing. Every inch of road was carefully watched during the twenty-mile trip. One bad bump could be a matter of life and death. But the ride was without incident. Kehoe's package was placed in a wide-open police yard. Plans were made to unseal the package the next day with every precaution possible put in place for diffusing a hidden bomb.[72]

◆ ◆ ◆

The sounds of vehicles, thousands it seemed, were heard throughout Bath. Headlamps of cars, trucks, and motorcycles lit up the roads leading into town, choked the streets, shone mercilessly past the homes of a town in shock and despair. Gawkers from throughout Michigan were coming to take a look. Between the powerful electrical lights at the school and the countless automobile head lamps, Bath was immersed in an unnatural light.

Ralph Cushman's body was transported from the morgue to a funeral home. Albert and Nellie wanted to be there, to spend the night, to be with their boy but instead became mired in a line of machines stretching down the roads. Traffic from emergency vehicles and gawkers was backed up for miles.

The Cushmans realized there was simply no getting to the funeral home in any decent amount of time. As darkness filled the skies, the steady beams of machine headlights cast an eerie glow.

At midnight, Albert and Nellie finally gave up, went home, and got in bed. Josephine crawled in with them. The family, now numbering three, hung on tight as if holding each other together. "They want to protect me," Josephine thought.[73]

Well into the early hours of May 19 the volunteers continued their herculean efforts. Electric lights powered by generators lit the scene as the rescue attempts continued through the night. The forms of workers cast jagged black shadows over the killing zone rubble.

Bricks and plaster were removed, piled with splintered wooden beams, roof tiles, broken glass, torn clothing, schoolbooks, children's desks, and chalkboards.

But no more bodies were found.[74]

When Ava Sweet went to school on May 18, it was a bright spring morning. Her day started sitting in class, one of twenty-six students in the sixth grade. In a matter of hours she was buried in rubble, rescued, taken to a Lansing hospital, released, and sent to stay with an aunt.

As night fell, only thirteen of her classmates were alive. No one was telling her anything about her brother Dean.[75]

Chapter 9

THE VALLEY OF THE SHADOW OF DEATH

Thursday morning, May 19. The sun rose over a killing zone.

School grounds littered with vestiges of the bombing. Buckets filled with blood-soaked rags. Coats and hats, shoes and socks like broken flowers strewn across the lawn. One girl's bloodstained coat and hat hanging from a tree limb. Schoolbooks, pages fluttering in the breeze. The inside of one book bore an anonymous student's warning: "Whoever touches this studies at his own risk."

There were piles of sheets, blankets, and other bedding used in triage and at the lawn morgue. Some of the bedclothes still bore dark imprints of children's bodies.[1]

Rubble from the north wing anchored the scene. Women and children gathered near the ruined building in prayer vigils.[2]

Throughout the day people came to the school, fetching coats, hats, books, and other items pulled from the rubble. Some of the clothes and books were returned to their owners; other items were given to grieving mothers and fathers.[3]

Area hospitals were flooded with offers from potential donors ready to provide any aid—money, blood, skin—to the victims.[4]

Fig. 13. An impromptu memorial. *(Courtesy of Tim Howery.)*

As Michigan's leader, Governor Green knew all eyes would be on him during the crisis and in the days that followed. The aftermath of the bombing raised innumerable questions, all underscored by one key element: money. A community was devastated. Medical supplies were desperately needed. Some parents could not afford to pay for funerals. Rubble had to be cleared away. None of these elements were cheap.

Furthermore, Bath needed a new consolidated school. The original facility was built at a cost of $43,000, with an additional $5,000 for equipment such as desks, books, lab materials, and other necessities. Only $8,000 had been paid back on bonds used to finance the school; another $1,200 had been added to the bill, the result of a loan granted to the school board just one month before. On the day of the bombing, the school board's coffers held only $188 in its general fund and $65 in the library fund.[5]

A meeting was held late Thursday in the governor's office with Rev. Edwin Bishop and William Smith. Both men ran local chapters of the American Red Cross, an ideal body to wrangle donations. It was decided that money for emergency relief would be funneled to the Red Cross; all other funds would go toward rebuilding the school. Green personally offered to pay the funeral expenses of families that could not afford proper burials for their children.[6]

After the meeting Governor Green issued a proclamation, appealing to the empathy and generosity of his constituency.

It is hardly possible to imagine a more terrible catastrophe than yesterday's at Bath. There is a little that we can do to lessen the grief of these stricken people. They have our boundless sympathy. While it is not given to us to assuage their grief, we can help in the material problem that confronts this community.

There has been a heavy expense cast upon them that I am sure the good people of Michigan will want to share. Besides the relief that we can give in individual cases, there is the restoration of their school house. The financial obligation on this small community of a new school house at this time is going to be very burdensome as the district is already heavily bonded. To assist in the relief work and to help in the matter of a new school building, I have appointed a committee headed by John W. Haarer of the City National Bank, Lansing, Michigan, to solicit and receive funds for this purpose. I believe that we will all feel better if we make a contribution to these people who have been so terribly stricken.[7]

Picking Haarer to head up the fund-raising relief committee was a smart choice. A former Michigan state treasurer, Haarer was a connected man now working as a vice president at the City National Bank of Lansing. Someone of his caliber was needed to make order out of the chaos of donations.

Unofficially, as noted in the *Lansing State Journal,* a relief effort began the day after the bombing "when Mrs. Franc D. C. Meyers sent a money donation to a local newspaper office, with an appropriate message asking that Michigan people contribute to the fund."[8]

There were no bounds to the kindness and generosity of strangers. The terrible deeds of one man produced a vast outpouring of public sympathy in the form of financial contributions.

Individuals sent checks, money orders, and cash. Businesses took up collections; schoolchildren brought in their nickels and pennies. "Not everyone can give a spectacular sum of money," said the *Journal,* "but many small contributions will exceed a large one, which will put a better aspect on the fund collected. The main consideration is the amount collected, but the more diversified the sources, the better the fund will seem to the people of Bath, who will then realize that sympathy is widespread and not isolated to a few wealthy people."[9]

Contributions were heavy throughout Michigan and surrounding states though donations certainly came from other parts of the country as well as Canada.

Charles Shean, warden at Michigan's Ionia Prison, announced that a group of inmates—murderers, rapists, and thieves of all sorts—had collected $200.00 for the cause.[10] Another institution, the Ingham County Tuberculosis Sanitarium, contributed $17.80, funds raised by children afflicted with the terrible lung disease.[11]

A pair of benefits was scheduled at movie theaters in nearby Mason and Williamston, with screenings of *Irene,* an early Technicolor feature starring Colleen Moore. The film print was provided free of charge and the local Kiwanis Clubs handled ticket sales with proceeds going to the Bath Relief Fund.[12]

Floyd Fitzsimmons, a Michigan boxing promoter, gifted with a big heart and a smart sense for good publicity, pledged 25 percent of the gate at the upcoming May 27 Detroit fight between lightweights Phil McGraw and Clicky Clark. (For the record, McGraw won in a decision.)[13]

On a tonier plane, the Tecla Pearl Corporation, of New York City, respected throughout the world for its elegant jewelry, offered a percentage of all the money it made from May 26 through May 28 at its Fifth Avenue shop. Another New Yorker sent a telegram announcing that he was raising money to help rebuild the school.[14]

The fund-raising effort received an unexpected but welcome charge from Washington when Senator James J. Couzens, Michigan's popular Republican representative, heard of the bombing.

Couzens ("pronounced exactly as 'cousins,'" he liked to say) was Canadian bred but Michigan devoted. Born on August 6, 1872, in Ontario, he moved to Detroit at age eighteen. Couzens worked low-level jobs for railroad and coal firms, saved his money, and invested wisely, becoming an early supporter of Henry Ford's automobile factory. In 1919, he sold his interest back to the Ford family, netting a phenomenal profit of thirty-five million dollars. Couzens then turned his attention to politics and was elected mayor of Detroit. In 1922, when Senator Truman H. Newberry was pushed into resignation (his fellow members of the U.S. Senate disapproved of Newberry's extravagant spending in his 1918 campaign against Couzens' former partner Henry Ford), Couzens was appointed to fill out the term. It was a popular choice; Couzens was easily elected for a full term two years later.[15]

Although his public life was marked by considerable achievement, the senator's personal life was shadowed by tragedy. Couzens and his wife Margaret had four children. One later served in his father's old office as Detroit's mayor, but two died under tragic circumstances. Their first child passed away as an infant. Their second son, Homer Couzens, died at age fourteen, killed after his Model T Ford—a birthday gift from his father—was wrecked.[16]

As if to atone for these heartbreaks, Couzens donated considerable sums to children's causes. His gift of ten million dollars established the Children's Fund of Michigan, a charity commissioned to help the poor receive free health and dental care. He established a foundation providing loans to the physically handicapped and gave freely to Michigan colleges and universities.[17]

A man of means with a strong sense of community, Couzens was deeply affected by Bath's tragedy. On Friday he wired Governor Green. "My sincere sympathies go out to the people of Bath in their great trouble," read the telegram. "Through you I offer any financial assistance that you desire whether in the interests of the parents or the children who lost their loved ones or in the rebuilding of the school."[18]

Initially the governor felt that Senator Couzens should be dealing with Haarer. Governor Green's original response was to put the senator in touch with "the committee in charge who will communicate with you." A sense of tact, coupled with political expediency, wisely intervened. Green scrapped his first draft, instead sending Couzens a telegram reading, "Your sympathy and generosity in offering financial assistance incident to catastrophe at Bath is greatly appreciated by all the people of Michigan. You have done a fine thing and we are all proud of you."[19]

Behind the scenes Green and Haarer grew worried. Although money poured in for the relief funds, they were concerned that Couzens's substantial coffers might deter other potential donors. It was a difficult juggling act, balancing political etiquette with the desperate need for money.

Haarer pulled it off with a public statement on Saturday, the day after Couzens's donation, as noted in the *Lansing State Journal.*

Two points were stressed by Mr. Haarer Saturday afternoon. The first is that every contribution is entirely voluntary. There has been no solicitation, and there will be none. It is thought that many Lansing companies and large corporations from which nothing has been received are waiting for a delegation to arrive with a formal request for money. The only request that anyone in Lansing will ever see will be in daily newspapers. The gifts must be spontaneous and quick for relief is needed, and cash must be forthcoming.

The second point emphasized by the chairman of the fund was that just because Sen. James Couzens telegraphed that he would extend any financial assistance that was thought necessary is no reason for everyone else dropping all plans for contributions. Senator Couzens has never said that he would shoulder the entire load. It was pointed out by Mr. Haarer, who also mentioned that it would be a gesture of very poor grace to assume that because he would be able to do this, if necessary, that therefore, he should be allowed to do so.[20]

Yet in the wake of Senator Couzens's offer, the fears of Governor Green and Haarer seemed to be realized. Donations to the Bath Relief Fund slowed over the next month; Haarer pointed to Couzens's deep-pocketed contribution as the cause.[21] As time passed, it was hard to say whether the senator's generosity had led to the gradual winding down of donations from individuals and corporations.

◆　◆　◆

Taking no chances on bad publicity, Metropolitan Life Insurance authorized its Lansing office to "waive all formalities and pay any . . . claims that might arise out of the Bath school disaster."[22]

◆　◆　◆

There was little surprise when commencement exercises for Bath's high school graduates were canceled. Diplomas would be given to students without formal recognition.[23] It would be another fifty years before the class of 1927 would take part in a graduation ceremony.

◆　◆　◆

Sheriff's deputies and other lawmen were dispatched throughout Bath to conduct a cautionary search. Did Kehoe plant more time bombs? Stores and public buildings, barns and some houses were scoured for anything that had the appearance of a wired alarm clock or errant dynamite.

Nothing was found.[24]

Kehoe's package, held overnight at the State Police headquarters, was held outside in a wide-open space. Keeping the box indoors risked damage and death within another building. No chances were being taken. For all intents and purposes, the box was a live bomb.

Lieutenant Lyle Morse and T. E. Trombla, an inspector with the explosives unit of the Interstate Commerce Commission in Detroit, were assigned to open Kehoe's package. Trombla knew his stuff; he had already looked over both the school and the Kehoe farm, providing his expertise to investigators.

They approached the crate carefully and gingerly removed the lid. Slowly light spilled inside.

No dynamite went off.

The box contained a set of ledger books and a simple note.

Dear Sir,

I am leaving the school board and turning over to you all my accounts. They are all in this box. Due to an uncashed check, the bank had 22¢ more than my books showed when I took them over. Due to an error on the part of the Secretary in order No. 118, dated Nov. 18, 1925 (He changed the figures on the order after the check had been sent to the payee), the bank gained one cent more over my books, making the bank account show 23¢ more than my books. Other wise I am sure you will find my books exactly right.

I thank you for going my bond.

Sincerely yours,
A. P. Kehoe

In his own way Kehoe proved himself a meticulous man to the end when it came to public finances.

But, stating that he was "leaving the school board" seemed like a twisted attempt at macabre humor, a dark and disturbing coda to his stenciled declaration that "Criminals Are Made, Not Born."[25]

◆ ◆ ◆

Newspapers throughout the country published a grotesque pencil rendering of Kehoe. This is the face of evil, editors collectively thundered. Look upon it with horror.

The picture bore only a passing resemblance to the man it represented. The real Andrew Kehoe was handsome with youthful features crowned by steel gray hair. His eyes were bright, and he had a rakish air about him. Photographs show a man who by looks alone could have been a banker, a businessman or a college professor, not a mass murderer.

The pencil sketch was otherwordly, resembling the creature in Mary Shelley's *Frankenstein,* a visual depiction of what Monty Ellsworth would call "the world's worst demon."[26] This Kehoe, as imagined by an anonymous artist, has a broad forehead and jutting cheekbones. His nose is more of a snout, long and triangular with porcine nostrils. The lips are thin, tight, and expressionless. His eyes, two black hollows shoved deep into the skull under heavy brows, are compelling. They glance to the side with a sense of melancholy, the ironic gaze of a haunted man.

◆ ◆ ◆

At the Kehoe farm, the natural aromas of the land mingled with the stench of smoke. Policemen combed the area. Nellie Kehoe had yet to be found.

A piece of paper lying near the remains of the Kehoe furniture caught the eye of A. R. Cournyer, one of the many people come to see the Bath wreckage and now roaming the burned farmland. He picked it up.

The scrap, written in what later was determined to be Kehoe's handwriting, was an ordinary shopping list with items any farmer might use. Both sides of the paper were filled. On the front Kehoe had written, "fuse, snaps, cotters 3/8, pump leathers, seed corn, potatoes." Beneath these items, in a different hand, were the words "Farm Bureau will send you the 20 bushels of yellow corn screenings."

The back of the paper completed Kehoe's shopping list. "Ammunition, plow points, 12 foot sash cord, telephone bill, watch, 2 pieces 1 ½ × 16 inch pipe, 3 threads, 1 ¾ inch, 45 degree bend, one 1 ¼ inch elbow, three pounds of putty."

The paper was undated.[27]

The State Police reassigned the rookie officer George Carpenter from the school site to Kehoe's farm. He and another policeman patrolled the area throughout the morning, then decided to take a well-deserved break for cigarettes.

They chose a space by the chicken coop. Nearby, they saw a cart. It wasn't really a cart, more like a makeshift wheelbarrow made out of a hog chute attached to a pair of wheels and a metal axle. How many people had passed this cart in the last thirty-six hours was hard to say. But

Fig. 14. The remains of Nellie Kehoe. *(Courtesy of the Bath School Museum.)*

by sheer chance Carpenter found what so many people were searching for.

Human remains, charred to the bone, lay in blackened repose on the cart. Nellie Kehoe finally was accounted for.[28]

Her left arm lay over the axle, completely loosened from the shoulder. The right was bent backward, bones fractured. It was impossible to tell if either of these limbs had been broken by human violence or fire.

Although both feet were burned away, Nellie's left toe was simply scorched; others were more or less intact. The body apparently had been dressed; fabric remains were found where the arm lay across the axle and corset stays littered the body.

Nellie's skull was cracked at the forehead. It was possible this break was the result of the fire; under extreme heat a human brain will expand and turn to gas until the skull gives way.

The other cause of this crack could have been a blow from a blunt instrument. Because the head was so badly charred, determining how Nellie's skull had been broken was impossible. Regardless, it was assumed by many—members of the inquest jury, legal authorities, newspaper writers, and Nellie's family and neighbors—that Kehoe had bludgeoned his wife then moved her body to where it was found.

A small piece of flesh and hair was still intact at the back of the skull.

Personal items were found with the body, laid gently with Nellie as if placed in ceremonial positions. Silverware was next to her head and atop her chest. A metal box, about a foot long, was beside the body. It wasn't a big box, maybe eight inches across and three inches deep, the kind of thing used to hold items for safekeeping.

Some objects inside probably had personal meaning. A lady's gold watch. A brooch and chain. Earrings. Two rings, one opal, one diamond. A dozen teaspoons with a *K* on each handle. A pin from the Knights of the Macabees, a social organization with considerable membership throughout Michigan.

Badly singed papers were also found inside the box. A marriage license. Statements and bills from the Saint Lawrence Hospital in Lansing and Henry Ford Hospital in Detroit.

And a large roll of what was either money or uncashed Liberty Bonds left over from the Great War, now burned so badly it was hard to tell which of the two currencies it was.[29]

Did Andrew Kehoe know about these funds? Could the money or bonds have covered his debts? It was another secret Kehoe—and Nellie—took to their graves.

◆ ◆ ◆

The pilgrimage of sightseers that began on the afternoon of May 18 continued into the next day and all through the weekend. It wouldn't slow down for months. The curious and the ghoulish alike came to catch a glimpse of the school, to tramp through the grounds of Kehoe's blackened farm.

It was overwhelming, long lines of black cars snaking along the roads into town, choking the air with gasoline fumes. Honking horns and chattering voices developed into a nonstop cacophony. The small town, which wasn't used to many automobiles in the first place, was jampacked by the nonstop parade.

Within hours of the explosion, the line of people wanting to see the ruins followed ambulances and other emergency vehicles. They came

Fig. 15. Onlookers viewing the cart where Nellie Kehoe was found.
(Photograph by Fred A. Stevens.)

throughout the night and into the morning, nonstop it seemed to an already emotionally overwhelmed town. By weekend, the traffic caused backups that ran for miles. State Police officers switched duties from rescue and cleanup to traffic control. Lansing police and county sheriff's deputies also helped to steer the lines.[30]

The influx of sightseers turned into an epic, albeit macabre, pilgrimage. One officer counted 2,750 machines pass by his watch in the course of just two hours. In downtown Bath, 173 automobiles were seen in the space of fifteen minutes. On Sunday alone, an estimated 85,000 cars passed through town.[31]

And they kept coming. The train between Bath and Lansing ran steadily, packed from door to door, window to window, with the curious.[32]

Kehoe's ruined farm was popular with the mobs. There was something compelling about the sight, a hypnotic attraction of evil that drew wave after wave of viewers. Thousands tramped through the grounds, paying no heed to the possibility that there might be unexploded dynamite on the premises.

The favorite—if macabre—attraction on the farm was the roped off cart where Nellie Kehoe's charred remains were found. People reached across the flimsy barrier to touch the large spoked wheels, tentatively grazing their fingers across the rims as if they were mystical portals into Kehoe's dark psyche.[33]

And still they kept coming. At daybreak on Sunday, the roads were clogged. Come three that afternoon, the traffic stretched out for nine miles from the town center. Machines weren't moving at all, just waiting, waiting for the morbid parade to inch its way into Bath, grab a peek, then slowly retreat out of town. The traffic, jammed in all directions, turned into a good-sized city of motor vehicles; one Sunday estimate put the crowd at more than fifty thousand. Accidents were inevitable. Fender benders were common, and there were some larger smashups. In one case a rear-end collision sent a child to the hospital; his stomach was sliced open in the crash.[34]

The State Police, by now used to wrangling the epic traffic, finally got orders: stop this foolishness. Red Cross workers from Lansing couldn't get through. A trip between Lansing and Bath took up to four hours, and even that was with a motorcycle escort.

State Police sent to the peripheries of the tourist lines told people to turn around. Go home. Get out.[35]

Chapter 10

REQUIEMS

So many dead. So much suffering. So many unrequited appeals to God. In hopes of providing answers, an anonymous individual donated red-covered Bibles to the parents of each dead child.[1]

The funerals were next.

An initial plan was made to hold a communal funeral service for the children. "[B]ent parents and forlorn relatives will wrap themselves in reticent black, and follow some 50 small caskets to the graveyard for the commencement of eternity for the school children and for the commencement of an era of bleak memories for the village," wrote Ted Christie, a "staff correspondent" for the *Lansing State Journal.*[2]

But realistically a mass funeral just wasn't practical. There simply were too many details in preparing the dead for burial to coordinate something of this magnitude.

Furthermore, many of the families wanted privacy in their mourning.

The large number of dead required an unusual amount of undertakers. The local funeral parlor in Bath couldn't handle all the work. Each body required care with an attention to detail that demanded time, patience, and empathy, something that needed to be done quickly but not at the expense of sensitivity.

The overflow of bodies went to funeral homes in Saint Johns, Laingsburg, and other nearby hamlets. William DeVinney, a sexton overseeing the burials at Pleasant Hill Cemetery, required extra grave diggers; one crew wasn't enough to excavate the ground for seventeen graves in time for all the funerals to be held there.[3]

Pallbearers were also in short supply. Neighbors volunteered their services in the grim task. Over the next three days Fordney Hart served at four funerals. "You try to get pole barers [sic] for forty-five people in a community that size and you have a problem," he later said. "You can't use any parents; you can't use any brothers and sisters. Some of the brothers and sisters were in the hospital anyhow."[4]

The Reverend Scott McDonald, normally a stoic presence at such somber occasions, didn't preside at most of the funeral services, but that was understandable. He, too, had lost a child in the bombing, his eldest daughter, eight-year-old Thelma. But McDonald did his best to fulfill his duties as the town's pastor, consoling grieving parents just as they consoled him.

His daughter was among the first children buried, just two days after the explosion. The McDonald home was strewn with wildflowers, a tribute picked from the woods and brought to the house by Thelma's surviving classmates.[5]

One person standing near McDonald saw the reverend holding his hands behind his back, digging his fingernails deep into his wrists. It was as if McDonald needed some kind of physical pain to counter the wounds inside.[6]

Another child's funeral hit a personal note at the *Lansing State Journal*. "Perhaps the hardest news story that [our] correspondent at Bath, Mrs. Le Vere [Florence] Harte, ever telephoned to this office, was transmitted Friday morning. It was related to the funeral arrangements for her own son, Robert, killed in the consolidated school blast." The article soberly gave the details, noting that "the officiating minister, Rev. S. B. McDonald, of Bath, will have full appreciation of the loss to the Hartes for the reason that he buried his own eldest daughter, Thelma, 8 years old, Friday morning at 10 o'clock."[7]

Funerals were done in shifts, as though to accommodate mourners so they could support one another. A family would bury its child in the morning, then attend another child's funeral in the afternoon.

It was a busy schedule. Most services were conducted in the home, as was the custom, though other memorials were held in either churches or funeral parlors in nearby towns.

Friday

Thelma McDonald, ten o'clock
Emerson Medcoff, ten o'clock
Elizabeth Witchell, ten o'clock
Arnold Baurele, two o'clock
Russell Chapman, 2:30
Earl Ewing, two o'clock
Galen Hart, two o'clock
Elise Robb, two o'clock
Cleo Clayton, three o'clock
Forrest Robert Cochran, time unknown
Emory Huyck, superintendent, time unknown

Saturday

Marjory Fritz, ten o'clock
Doris Johns, ten o'clock
Robert Hart, two o'clock
Clarence McFarren, ten o'clock
Pauline Shirts, ten o'clock
Catherine Foote, 10:30
Blanche Hart, teacher, eleven o'clock
Ralph Cushman, one o'clock
Floyd Burnett, 1:30
Emilie and Robert Bromund, 1:30
Stanley Hart, 1:30
Emma Nichols, 1:30
Nelson McFarren, retired, and Glenn Smith, postman, two o'clock
George and Willa Hall, two o'clock
Francis Hoeppner, two o'clock
Richard Richardson, 2:30

Sunday

Loren Huster, two o'clock
Carlyle Geisenhaver, two o'clock
Lemoyne Woodman, two o'clock
Iola, Vivian, and Percy Hart, 2:30
George and Lloyd Zimmerman, 2:30

Henry and Herman Bergan, time unknown
Hazel Weatherby, teacher, time unknown

The *Lansing State Journal* referred to Bath as "a valley of tears," an apt description. On Friday, the Reverend George Woolcock, a Baptist minister from Grand Rapids, conducted the funeral service for eleven-year-old Earl Ewing. His voice slowly grew faint during the sermon. Woolcock's throat tightened. He paused, then stopped, tried again but could not continue.

As Ewing's casket was carried to the hearse, the crowd of spectators come to see the sights fell silent, a brief moment of respect within the strange parade of humanity that had invaded Bath in the past forty-eight hours. Reverend Woolcock walked protectively next to the casket. His face was wet with tears.[8]

Three wreaths and three crepe ribbons hung somberly on Eugene Hart's home, one for each of their children killed: nine-year-old Vivian, eleven-year-old Percy, and Iola, who would have turned thirteen one month and one day after she was killed.[9] Seventeen-year-old Perry still clung to life, chunks of iron deeply lodged in his foot. Shoe leather and materials from his socks were also embedded in his flesh.[10]

To the quiet horror of those in mourning, the tourists destroyed any sense of privacy in grief. Families that had multiple funerals to attend were constantly running late, unable to negotiate the massive crowds by foot, horse, or car. Onlookers thronged the streets watching hearses struggle on their journeys from funeral home to house of mourning and finally cemetery. State Police officers did the best they could to help restore some dignity to a grief-stricken people. One clergyman, hopelessly caught up in the snarled traffic, piggybacked a ride on a state trooper's motorcycle in order to preside over a funeral. After the lawman dropped him off, the minister turned around to fetch Ada Belle Mead and Sadie Drumheller, two middle-aged sisters known for their church singing who now were providing emotional hymns for many funerals.

The insidious noise of cars and people filtered from the streets into the homes of mourners. Perhaps the Hart family suffered the most. During the funeral service for their three children, a throng of curious onlookers lined the sidewalk. Those inside the house often strained to hear the eulogy delivered by Reverend L. H. Ledford; his words of comfort were consistently undercut by car horns, roaring engines, the screech of wheels, and other agonizingly loud traffic noises.[11]

Yet the people of Bath kept their civility regardless of any tactless actions or requests. One driver called out to a woman on the side of the road, asking for directions to the cemetery. The tourist was interested in seeing where the children would be laid to rest.

"Just down the road a way," she responded. Her eyes brimmed with tears. "That's where I'm burying two children tomorrow."[12]

Other visitors were more brazen in their requests. Paying no attention to tact, decorum, or basic decency, morbidly curious people disregarded mourning families and peeked through doorways or windows. These Peeping Toms had one thing in common: they wanted to see the dead children up close.[13]

One family, lost in its sorrow, answered a random knock at the door. "I want to see the dead body," demanded the unwanted visitor.

The request was denied.[14]

In the Cushman house, Ralph lay in a casket lined with white silk. Nellie gently placed a red tulip in his hands.

She had picked the flower from where it grew next to the front porch. For the longest time, Ralph had begged to have the tulip; Nellie had always given him a firm no.

The time had come to let Ralph have the tulip.[15]

Josephine felt different that day. I'm not a kid anymore, she thought. I'm more grown up now, more *something*.

Her childhood, she realized, had vanished.[16]

The house overflowed with the aroma of flowers. So many had been sent to the Cushmans that their home seemed like something of an indoor garden. One aunt could only find sweet peas, a wide variety of pinks that added a unique splash of color to the somber plethora of bouquets and floral arrangements.

One of the volunteer ministers, a pastor from a Baptist church in Lansing, performed Ralph's funeral service. Ada Belle Mead and Sadie Drumheller sang "Rock of Ages" a cappella. Albert, Nellie, and Josephine stood stoically at Ralph's casket surrounded by family, surrounded by friends, surrounded by prayer.

When the service was over, Ralph and Leon Carrier, Albert's uncle and cousin, took the Cushmans to the cemetery. The small coffin was lowered into the grave; more prayers were said. Ralph, tulip in his hands, was covered with the rich brown earth.

Finally Nellie Cushman wept.[17]

A delegation from the Lansing branch of the U.S. Postal Service came to Glen Smith's funeral on Saturday. Mailmen, accompanied by other postal workers and officials, brought with them a large floral arrangement honoring their fallen colleague.[18]

Emory Huyck's funeral was held on Friday in Carson City, Michigan, the town where he was born and where his parents still lived. Having been a loyal Mason throughout his adult life, Huyck's funeral was planned by the Carson City Masonic Lodge. John Setherington, the worshipful master of the lodge conducted the service. A school superintendent from a nearby district spoke of Huyck's dedication to learning. A Methodist pastor gave the eulogy, taking his cue from the Twenty-third Psalm.

> The Lord is my shepherd: I shall not want.
> He maketh me to lie down in green Pastures, he leadeth me beside
> the still waters.
> He restoreth my soul: he leadeth me in the paths of righteousness for
> his name's sake,
> Yea, though I walk through the valley of the shadow of death, I will
> fear no evil: for thou art with me, thy rod and staff they comfort
> me.
> Thou preparest a table before me in the presence of mine enemies:
> thou annointeth my head with oil; my cup runneth over.
> Surely goodness and mercy shall follow me all the days of my life: and
> I will dwell in the house of the Lord for ever.[19]

On Saturday Roscoe Hart's home turned into a funeral parlor for his wife, Blanche, Bath Consolidated's fifth-grade teacher. She died just three weeks shy of the couple's eighth anniversary, on June 4. After the service, she was buried at Wilsey Cemetery just outside of town. Six of her former classmates served as pallbearers.[20]

◆ ◆ ◆

There were two other burials, both held on Friday.

A Catholic service was held for Nellie Price Kehoe at the Lansing Resurrection Church, presided over by Fr. John O'Rafferty. Two days before O'Rafferty had spoken at the Sparrow Hospital fund-raiser as the Bath disaster unfolded; now he delivered a funeral service for one of its most prominent victims. One hundred relatives and friends attended the memorial. On their way into the church, the mourners were confronted by a few newspaper photographers. Words were exchanged, and a scuffle nearly broke out between the grieving and the newsmen.

Throughout his sermon, Father O'Rafferty didn't refer directly to the way Nellie's life ended. Yet he closed his sermon with words of forgiveness, quoting a dying Jesus from Luke 23:24.

"Forgive them, Father, for they know not what they do."

Forgiveness was a hard accomplishment after the funeral. Having retreated from the church entrance, the news photographers now ensconced themselves across the street, poking their lenses from a second-story window overlooking the funeral procession. Friends of the Price family picked up the fight that had started before the service, storming the building and confronting the photographers.[21]

Nellie was laid to rest in the Price family plot at Lansing's Mount Hope Cemetery. Her headstone reads "Ellen A. Price 1875–1927."

Two hours before mass was said for Nellie Kehoe, the indistinct body parts of Andrew Kehoe were placed in a coffin, lowered into the ground, and covered with dirt. It was as anonymous as a burial could be.

Yet Kehoe's interment was marked by careful organization, done with a certain sense of ritualism albeit without sanctity or prayers. One of his sisters, now living in Battle Creek, Michigan, purchased a casket. On Thursday afternoon, workmen dug several graves at the Mount Hope Cemetery in Saint Johns in a section normally reserved for indigents. (There was profound irony in Andrew and Nellie Kehoe's final resting places both being named "Mount Hope Cemetery.") Numerous holes were dug as a ruse to confuse would-be vigilantes eager to take revenge on Kehoe's corpse.

Although there had been some talk of burying Kehoe in a family plot, his surviving relatives agreed that this anonymous internment was for the best. The pauper's section of Mount Hope—like any other potter's field—was stuck in an out-of-the-way corner. It looked like an afterthought in the graveyard, an area without much greenery or funerary monuments. The undertaker and a couple of grave diggers chose one of the holes, lowered the casket, and covered it with yellow-brown earth.

The other holes were filled in as well. Later, when he was asked to point out Kehoe's grave, the cemetery's sexton was at a loss.[22]

Although plans for Kehoe's funeral weren't made public, a pair of newspapermen managed to find out the time and place. They lurked across the street, shadowy figures seemingly stuck with an assignment no one in the newsroom cared to take on. One man left; the other stuck around for a few hours to see if anything might happen.

He wasn't disappointed. After a time, two cars pulled into the potter's field. No one exited either auto; the machines simply flanked the grave. The occupants included one of Kehoe's sisters and his only brother plus a few old friends.

After a few moments, the machines pulled away. The business of disposing of Andrew P. Kehoe's remains was over.[23]

◆ ◆ ◆

Throughout the weekend ministers carefully prepared sermons, trying to find answers to agonizing questions within the comfort of scripture. In nearby Okemos, Rev. V. B. Niles announced that he would deliver a homily to his congregation titled "Tragedy's Need."[24]

Rev. Edwin Bishop, so personally involved through his fund-raising work with the governor, as well as serving as one of the many ministers on call for victims' funerals, faced his congregation at Plymouth Congregational Church. He had spent many hours thinking through his emotional chasm.

The pastor looked deep into his faith for answers. Now it was time to share with his flock.

"In many a picture gallery in Europe," he began, "there hangs an artist's representation of the 'Massacre of the Innocents.' The gruesome portrayal of Herod's brutal soldiers tearing little children from their agonized mothers' arms and then putting them to the sword has been spread upon canvas. It is a pitiful picture, as it was a pitiful reality. And now we have had our own massacre of the innocents, right here in Michigan, in a peaceful country hamlet, on a beautiful May morning, in a building dedicated by the community to growing youth the perpetrator thereof being from that group supposed to represent the substantial backbone of our population. Like the wreck of the Titanic, the rending, crashing blow came from the unseen and the unsuspected."

Through vivid language, Bishop relived the tragedy for his flock. "After 1900 years, in Bath, in Michigan, is repeating the experience of Bethlehem in Judea—'A voice was heard in Ramah, weeping and great mourning, Rachel weeping for her children and refusing to be comforted because they were not.' Because of all the circumstances, the Bath tragedy in our own neighborhood is likely to be known the world over as *sui generis*."

Throughout his sermon, Bishop seemed to be searching for answers to the big question of "why." He looked at all aspects of Kehoe, considering nature versus nurture, criminal psychology, and what he termed "the hazards of modern civilization." "[T]he nervous and mental strain of our high-speed living are all taking mortal toll," he continued. "It is particularly uncertain today that when the family leaves the breakfast table in the morning they will all foregather again at night."

Kehoe's crimes were beyond reason, beyond any kind of normal explanation. "Would that a Nathaniel Hawthorne could write this case up!" he declared. Yet, he concluded, the unadulterated evil of one man's deeds inevitably brought out the best of humanity. "Hate had its hour in Bath, but love followed quickly at hate's heels," he told the congregation.[25]

◆ ◆ ◆

With three children vanquished and a fourth critically injured, Eugene Hart and his wife held the dubious distinction of being the family suffering the deepest losses. It was a loss in which words of comfort were useless.

Yet from somewhere deep inside, the Harts found words of appreciation, which they published in a small and eloquent ad taken out in the "Announcements" section of the local newspaper. "We desire to express our heart-felt thanks to our many friends and neighbors, to our governor and Mrs. Green, to all women societies, to the doctors and nurses and the Red Cross, to our police of Lansing and state, to our business men of Lansing, and all neighboring cities and towns, to unknown friends and sympathizers in other states and cities, in general to all nearby and far who aided and comforted us in this, the dark hour of our lives. Mr. and Mrs. Eugene Hart, Bath, Michigan."[26]

The Bauerle family also placed a notice thanking their many friends and "any more unknown to us who cared for our 'Dear Arnold' during his last moments of suffering."[27]

◆ ◆ ◆

On Wednesday, during their chance meeting on the street, Kehoe had told Albert Detluff that the next school board meeting was scheduled for Friday, May 20. So it was.

They came to the Community Hall, the trustees, faces drawn and weary. Some of their children were dead; some of their children were injured. All had friends suffering devastating losses.

Newsmen filled the room. There was a dark anticipation in the air. Surely something had to be said about the bombing. It certainly would make for good copy. William Searl was there, too, a somber figure with heavy duties.[28]

The meeting's minutes, handwritten in a simple ledger, are starkly bureaucratic. All business, there is nothing in the report that reflects the tragedy. "Meeting called to order by the president of the board," it reads. "Officers present G. Morris G. O. Spangler A. Detluff and M. W. Kyes."

The next line states that the minutes of the last meeting, held on May 2, were read. The first item on the record was a motion to advance Detluff, the board's purchasing agent, twenty-five dollars to pay a small bill.

The motion, which carried, was made by "A. P. Kehoe."[29]

The next piece of business was the appointment of a new treasurer. An offer made to J. W. Webster, a longtime board member, was respectfully declined. It was understandable. Webster was a chicken farmer and shock waves from the blast had destroyed the twenty-four thousand eggs in his incubators.[30]

Another name came up: former school board treasurer Enos Peacock, the man Kehoe defeated in the 1924 elections. Peacock was telephoned with the offer. He agreed to take the position. Someone drove through the sightseeing hordes, picked Peacock up, and returned to the meeting so the new treasurer could be officially sworn in.

None of this is reflected in the minutes, which read simply, "Moved by M. W. Kyes Enos Peacock be appointed teasuer [*sic*] of School carried." [31]

Searl administered the oath of office, and the board moved to other issues. Was the board liable for the losses—both life and property—incurred in the bombing? It was suggested that the Michigan attorney general's office be consulted; ultimately it was decided to wait for the results of the pending inquest.

Funding the rebuilding of the school was another concern. Money was tight. It was noted that the ledgers for May listed nearly $3,300.00 in debits and $128.04 in the treasury. Nearly $40,000.00 in bonds were still owed on the school building. Unless there was considerable help from the state or other sources, a dire financial crisis loomed over the school board.[32]

They turned to the question of replacing the devastated property. Should the school be rebuilt on the same site? Perhaps the building should be razed, the land turned into a memorial park, and a new school be built elsewhere. Nothing, of course, could be decided at the moment.[33] It would take years of healing and a new generation of board members to answer these questions.

A new superintendent, Harry Brandt, was approved as Huyck's replacement, an appointment steeped in irony. Brandt's official hiring was mere formality. Having decided to move on in his career, Huyck had earlier submitted his resignation. Surely Kehoe must have been aware of this development.[34]

Another administrative hiring was approved: Frank Ray would be the new principal. Like Huyck, Floyd Huggett had previously resigned from his job. These two administrative changes were expected.

Hiring replacement teachers for the late Blanche Harte and Hazel Weatherby would have to wait.[35]

Detluff moved that the meeting be adjourned. The motion carried.[36]

With their official monthly duties completed, the trustees departed into the night.

IN THE MATTER OF THE INQUEST AS TO THE CAUSE OF DEATH OF EMERY E. HUYCK, DECEASED

William Searl, prosecuting attorney for the county, initially planned the inquest for Thursday morning at nine o'clock, just twenty-four hours after the bombing. He quickly realized this would be a terrible mistake. The dead were not yet buried. Potential witnesses undoubtedly would be consumed with grief and suffering from physical exhaustion.[1]

Yet an informal hearing—what the *Lansing State Journal* referred to as "John Doe proceedings"—was held late Thursday afternoon.[2] Six men, chosen from the hasty pool Searl compiled on Wednesday, were sworn into service as jurors: Alton Church, Wilmer Coleman, Edward Drumheller, Ishmell Everett, Clarence Tolman and Burt Wilcox. They were selected in part for their highly respected status within the community. Additionally, each man had no children. While the men certainly mourned for their family and friends, none would be swept by the grief of losing a son or daughter. Theoretically the six would have open minds when sifting through the evidence presented to them.[3]

Officially the jurors were responsible for a single task: learn all the details leading up to the death of Superintendent Huyck. Everything up to and following Kehoe's murder-suicide, including motivation, wiring the school, setting fire to his property, and killing Nellie, were part of the process. Deriving an account of what led to May 18 and how the day played out was an unspoken goal of the inquest.

As farmer-cum-coroner, C. E. Lamb was dependent on Searl to run the proceedings. County coroner was an elected position with duties that included death investigations caused by unusual circumstances. But Lamb was a farmer, not a legal scholar. With so many dead under such extraordinary conditions, he faced an inquest that was simply unprecedented. With Searl in command, Lamb surely felt considerable relief.

The proceedings were held in the ballroom of the Community Hall. Normally a gathering place for dances or amateur theatrics, the space was outfitted with two tables in front of the ballroom stage. One table was for jurors, the other for called witnesses. It was a stark setting, lit only by a few bare bulbs dangling off wires strung from the ceiling. Small windows on either side of the ballroom provided a little more illumination, but overall the setting reflected the sober nature of the gathering.[4]

Relatively few witnesses appeared at the preliminary investigation. Janitor Frank Smith gave brief testimony. Six weeks previously he'd found the broken lock on the school door. Yes, he said, Kehoe had a key to the building for access anytime he needed it. And over the past week doors within the basement, normally shut, were found open.[5]

Although the initial proceedings went unrecorded, Chief Charles Lane spoke with the press afterward, providing a hint of what was to come during the official hearing, now scheduled for Monday morning.

No evidence, he said, was presented suggesting that anyone but Kehoe was behind the bombing. The wiring, while not completely examined, conceivably could have been accomplished by one man. For now, people would have to wait for answers.[6]

To some, the proceedings were senseless. Nothing could bring back the children; at best, the hearing might cauterize a psychic wound by explaining Kehoe's actions. For many still deep in shock, such a prospect offered little—if any—comfort.

◆ ◆ ◆

Fifty-five witnesses were called over two days, a cross section of students, school employees, board members, rescue workers, attorneys, and Kehoe's neighbors (the term "Kehoe's friends" didn't seem apt). Glenn

Whitman, a talented court reporter, took down each word spoken by Searl and the witnesses. They told their stories in simple, unadorned English. There was no need for embellishment.

The tale unfolded in bits and pieces. Kehoe's strange behavior on Wednesday morning. The first sounds of an explosion at the school. How the ground trembled. What people saw, what people did. Children's low moans and high screams emerging from the rubble. A fledgling rescue effort. Huyck's devotion to duty, seemingly everywhere in those early moments, running from the school to triage to deathbeds and back to the school.

The fire at Kehoe's farm. Its rapid spread. Kehoe in his machine, emerging from the smoke, telling people to go to the school. ("I knew when he gave that warning possibly there might be something doing," Sydney Howell testified.)[7]

How Kehoe pulled up to the school. Calling Huyck to his truck. The second explosion. Terror. Panic.

Wiring, blasting caps, and dynamite winding with deadly precision throughout the labyrinthine underworld of the Bath Consolidated School. Dynamite in the Kehoe house, timers, and wiring leading to his farm buildings.

Horses hobbled by wire, roasted and burned alive. Searching for Nellie. Discovering her body and personal artifacts.

Background information. Kehoe's antagonistic relationship with Huyck. His obstinate refusal to pay the mortgage. Nellie's illnesses. Her last hours.

Kehoe's talents. Mechanical. Electrical. Psychological. Unlimited access to the school. Time to develop a plan for destruction. Patience and diligence over the course of weeks or months, working in cramped, darkened spaces, gently pushing material into place, working through the night, bit by bit, piece by piece, until each element was in place.

The story unfolded over two days, a mosaic of memory and eyewitness accounts, physical evidence, and documentation. An undercurrent of extreme violence contrasted with unembellished heroism was laced together by the pastiche of stories.

And then it was over.

"Gentlemen," said Searl, "we have no other witnesses here, and we expect to close the Inquest unless there is some other question you want answered, or unless you know of some other witnesses, or unless there are some other witnesses in the room that know about this. I think that is all then, Gentlemen. I think you can go down in the basement to deliberate on this."[8]

The results didn't take long. After a short deliberation, the six-man jury delivered its findings. Kehoe had acquired dynamite to carry out an elaborate plan. He had killed his wife, blown up the school and burned down his own farm with timers, driven to Bath, and blown up his truck to murder Huyck.

"We find that the said Andrew P. Kehoe was sane at all times, and so conducted himself and concealed his operations that there was no cause to suspicion any of the above acts," read the concluding lines, "and we further find, that the School Board, and Frank Smith, Janitor of said school building, were not negligent in and about their duties, and were not guilty of any negligence in not discovering said plan."[9]

◆ ◆ ◆

Lacing the school with explosives, murdering his wife, setting his farm ablaze, blowing himself up, killing forty-four all told (including Nellie and himself), these were unthinkable crimes that *could* be explained by "how." The "why" remained elusive.

The general explanation, as retold in countless newspaper articles, in history books, and on Web pages, is that Kehoe was angry over property taxes and the possibility of losing his home. On the surface, that seems too simple, too pat an answer for the level of horror inflicted. Taxes are never a neutral issue; on any given day in any given place in any given period of history, people have complained and acted on government taxation. Like his father before him, Kehoe zealously spoke out against taxes, but they were hardly alone in this respect.

People upset over taxes do many things, but the systematic planning and realization of multiple, large-scale bombings by one person is on a psychological level far beyond anger.

The historical record shows that Kehoe was in no danger of being forced out of his home; the attorney Joseph Dunnebacke stated as much during the inquest, although this was a theory quickly postulated by newspapers in the wake of the bombing. "At no time did the executors of the Price Estate press Andrew Kehoe for his money," Dunnebacke told the jurors. . . . "On the contrary, it was my idea, and I am sure Mr. Kehoe so understood it, that he would be given every opportunity to work out his problem by making a sale of his farm and thereby saving his equity."[10] It stood to reason that the Price sisters would not be so cruel and uncaring as to throw the Kehoes out of the house with Nellie so desperately ill.

Somewhere, somehow, some *thing* in Kehoe lost its way. No matter how much puzzling and questioning there is, the real answer—Kehoe's personal "why"—burned to ash with his farm, exploded into senseless matter with his flesh, and was wiped from the earth at his own willing. The wooden suicide note found at the edge of his farm gives a clue. What happened in Bath, he seemed to be telling the world, was created by others. As the Virginia Tech shooter Seung-Hui Cho would claim about himself years later, Kehoe believed he was not personally responsible for the mayhem. It was the fault of others who had pushed him to the edge, turning Kehoe into a man for whom epic death and destruction was his last means of personal expression.

Psychology, the plaything of the leisure class, was all the rage during the 1920s. In sophisticated New York City, Greenwich Village Bohemians held "Freuding" parties with guests telling about and analyzing one another's dreams.[11] Three years before the bombing, in Chicago defense attorney Clarence Darrow had turned a disturbing light on unsettled minds in his defense of Nathan Leopold and Richard Loeb, two brilliant University of Chicago students who brutally murdered fourteen-year-old Bobby Franks just for the thrill of it. The prosecution demanded the death penalty. Darrow delved into the psychology of his clients in a determined effort to save their lives. "How insane they are I care not, whether medically or legally," he implored the judge. "They did not reason; they could not reason; they committed the most foolish, most unprovoked, most purposeless, most causeless act that any two boys ever committed. . . . They killed . . . because they were made that way. Because somewhere in the infinite processes that go to the making up of the boy or the man something slipped."[12]

During a staff dinner held at Owosso Memorial Hospital on May 21, three days after the bombing, a group of medical scientists gave their collective diagnosis of Kehoe's psychology. He was manic depressive, they claimed, a man who created and executed his plan as an escape from his depressed state. Kehoe's suicide, the doctors concluded, showed that he was not paranoid. A paranoid individual, convinced the world is out to get him, might kill others but certainly would not commit suicide.[13]

Decades after the bombing, there is a better understanding of what forces operated inside Kehoe's brain. *Psychopath* was a word tossed around in 1927 as easily as terms such as *masochist* or *Oedipus complex*. As a mental illness and motivator, psychopathic behavior is now recognized and diagnosed with clarity. There are unique characteristics of the disorder, as identified by Dr. Robert Hare, a Canadian professor of psychology and leading expert in this dark underworld of human behavior.

Hare finds similar traits in the psychopathic individual, be that person an office control freak, a con artist, or a killer. "The Hare Psychopathy Checklist," considered a "gold standard" indicator, zeroes in on specific behavioral factors that ultimately define who can be considered a psychopath. In Kehoe's case, the profile fits all too well. Among the checklist items he scores high on are glibness/superficial charm; grandiose sense of self-worth; pathological lying; conning/manipulative; lack of remorse or guilt; shallow affect; callous/lack of empathy; poor behavioral control; lack of realistic, long-term goals; failure to accept responsibility for own actions ("Criminals are made, not born"); and criminal versatility. Psychopaths, by Hare's standards, have a unique ability to lead a double life, respectable in public while maintaining a well thought out plan and cunning talents used to manipulate—and sometimes kill—their victims. "Psychopathic killers," writes Hare, "are not mad, according to accepted legal and psychiatric standards. Their acts result not from a deranged mind but from cold, calculating rationality combined with a chilling inability to treat others as thinking, feeling human beings. Such morally incomprehensible behavior, exhibited by a seemingly normal person, leaves us feeling bewildered and helpless."[14] Dr. Hare's words echo and amplify the findings of William Searl and the Bath inquest jurors: "We find that the said Andrew P. Kehoe was sane at all times, and so conducted himself and concealed his operations that there was no cause to suspicion."[15]

While it's tempting to play armchair psychoanalyst decades after the bombing, the reality is that in suicide Kehoe took the "why" of what he did with him. It's part of the mystery of who Andrew Kehoe was, something buried deep within a soul blown to pieces by its own compelling force.

Chapter 12

SUMMER

Ava Sweet was temporarily sent to live with her sister Clara in Lansing. No one talked with Ava about her younger brother Dean. In fact, no one seemed to want to talk about anything related to the school.

After a couple of days, Ava was told that her older sister, Florence Hart, was in mourning. Florence's son Robert—Ava and Dean's nephew—was among the dead. But still there was no word about her brother.

The silence about Dean drove Ava just about crazy. Day after day passed, and the topic remained taboo. She felt left out, as though the grownups were protecting her, shielding her from something terrible. Ava was empty inside and led her to one conclusion: Dean was dead.

About five days after the bombing she was finally told the truth. Dean wasn't dead but was clinging to life. In a coma. Her mother was keeping vigil by Dean's bedside. Her father, though wracked with concern over his children and mourning the loss of his grandson, had to keep going. May was always a busy time for Bath residents; like his neighbors, Willard Sweet had a dairy farm to run. Farmers could not afford to neglect land or animals.

The news, while providing the answers she hungered for, brought Ava no sense of satisfaction.

Ava had a problem of her own, though obviously it was not a matter of life or death. Her hair, thick with plaster dust, had to be washed time and again. A single shampooing simply couldn't do the trick; it took the better part of a week to wash all the dust out of her hair and scalp before Ava's shoulder-length bob was restored to its normal dark brown hue.[1]

◆ ◆ ◆

Kehoe's work was unprecedented. There was a public struggle, an awkward search for the exact words to describe what he had done. On May 27, the *Lansing State Journal,* in an editorial headlined "Bath Crime Suggests New Noun, New Verb," attempted to resolve the dilemma.

> Because the crime of Andrew Kehoe, dynamiter of the Bath Consolidated School, is the first of its kind, and therefore unique, it is believed, in at least modern times, no descriptive word has as yet been evolved which would indicate the character and quality of the act, if a similar one is ever perpetrated. A member of the *State Journal* editorial staff has therefore coined the verb "kehoe" to cover the situation. Applications of the idea would cause any person who destroys another or others by explosives to be termed a "kehoe," the act committed would be a "kehoe," while the victim would be considered as having been "kehoed."
>
> The word "burke," more familiar in the British Isles than in the United States, is a verb describing the act of murdering a person so as to leave no marks of violence. It was coined when William Burke, the first person known to have committed this crime, was executed for it in Edinburgh, Scotland, in 1829. He had sought to sell the body for dissection.[2]

Although "burke" remains a standard—albeit obscure—word in the English language, "kehoe" never made its way into the lexicon of criminal acts. It would be many years before the terror wave of splattered blood, broken bodies, and perpetrators packed with determination and explosives brought the term "suicide bomber" into the language to better describe "any person who destroys another or others by explosives."

◆ ◆ ◆

A week after the blast, in nearby Saint Johns, an older man garbed in ratty clothing and carrying a burlap sack rambled through the streets. When he reached the main business district, the man stood for a moment, then dropped his bundle to the sidewalk.

"Don't touch that sack," he warned anyone who came near. "There's dynamite in it."

In the wake of the news from Bath, people in Saint Johns took no chances. Sheriff Fox was sent for immediately. But Fox knew the man, Sid Stickney all too well. Stickney was often a temporary tenant of the Saint Johns jail. The would-be bomber was less inspired by Kehoe than he was by his unsteady mind.

Fox examined Stickney's baggage. He found no surprises. The "dynamite" turned out to be an old stovepipe, a few water basins, and a battered teakettle.

It was another night in jail for Sid Stickney.[3]

♦ ♦ ♦

On Sunday, June 19, the curious spilled into Bath once again, tramping through the remains of Kehoe's farm. Like the thousands who preceded them, these tourists stared with a mix of awe, horror, and cheap thrills at what remained of the devastated farm.

A perfect way to spend an early summer Sunday.

The milling of the crowd and the usual hushed tones were interrupted this day by a voice. Sidney J. Howell carried a rare distinction: he was a defender of Kehoe. The two men had been friends—as much as one could be friends with Kehoe—and Howell was deeply troubled by the actions of his late companion. In the weeks that followed the bombing, Sidney Howell turned over in his mind the pieces of Kehoe's crimes. How could his friend have done such a fiendish act? It just wasn't possible, not the Andrew Kehoe Howell knew.

Throughout his testimony during the inquest, Howell had struggled with the overwhelming evidence against Kehoe. Yes, he told the jurors, he noticed that Kehoe seemed "cooler" in the days before the explosion, less talkative and more introspective than usual. But the wiring around Kehoe's house could have been preparation for linking the farm to the coming Consumers Power resources. As for Mrs. Kehoe's burned body, Howell believed that Nellie had died and Kehoe—perhaps in an act of kindness—had placed her body outside for someone to find; her charred corpse might have been a complete accident. As for the timing device setting off the explosion, Howell believed it could have misfired and was meant to go off at the Parent-Teacher Association meeting the night of May 17. "He had no enmity toward the children, and I thought possibly he might have toward the people. In fact I never know him to have any hatred, be vindictive," Howell told the jurors.[4]

Something in Kehoe's psyche must have slipped, he decided, something so horrendous, so evil that the man whom Howell called "friend" underwent a Jekyll and Hyde transformation beyond human control. Emotions swept away Howell's better sensibilities. He took to the streets of Bath determined to clear Kehoe's name, a sort of defender of the dead, trying to salvage what he could of his late friend's reputation.

Howell's efforts didn't pass unnoticed, particularly by the legal authorities. Both Searl and Sheriff Fox warned him to watch his tongue lest he get into serious trouble.

It was no use. Howell maintained that he had the right to say what was on his mind whenever he wanted. "Free speech is every man's prerogative in this country," sniffed one newspaper editor, "but it may be carried too far, althoug[h] Howell evidently doesn't think so."[5]

So it was on this warm day on the remains of Kehoe's land. Howell began his speech. "Mr. Kehoe was such a fine man that he would never have done what he did unless he had been insane."

They were the only words Howell spoke. A man burst through the crowd, hands stretched out like the claws of a hawk closing in on its prey. Locals immediately recognized the avenger. His son was a broken survivor of the blast.

The hands clamped around Howell's neck. Someone managed to separate the two, probably saving Howell's life in the process. Howell was sent packing, his defense of Kehoe silenced at last.

Howell's loyalty to Kehoe made him a *persona non grata* in Bath. Anything he did with Kehoe in the past was immediately suspect. Howell's son had once borrowed a horse from Kehoe, you say? Well, it just goes to show you what kind of people those Howells are. One local woman was particularly ruthless in her gossip, saying anything and everything she could about the Howells regardless of its veracity.[6]

Howell may have lacked tact, but he certainly was a man who knew where he wasn't wanted. Eventually he moved out of town—where to no one seemed to know or care.

Howell left, but the talk remained. What kind of man was Howell to defend that monster Kehoe? What sick demons infested Howell's brain? Gone? Good!

Later word came back to Bath that Sidney Howell died when his automobile was hit by a train. The official record said his automobile smashed into a speeding train.[7] Rumors in Bath said otherwise. Some said the car was stuck on the tracks. Another story had Howell simply stopping his machine in front of an approaching locomotive and waiting for the inevitable.[8]

◆ ◆ ◆

Periodically letters, some signed, some anonymous would arrive in town. Many were expressions of sympathy, an outreach of humanity to a people wounded both physically and spiritually. Schoolchildren everywhere readily identified with Bath's dead. "Our teacher Mr. Egidio Barroni, has told us today of the tragedy that happened in your village, caused by the explosion of dynamite," wrote a class of seventh graders in Pisaro, Italy. "Even if we are far away, this terrible tragedy has left us an impression, our sorrow is too big and we feel that we ought to write with our hearts to the pains that the children must have suffered, and to the greater sorrow of the poor mothers. We want you to know that all Italy is sympathizing in your tears."[9]

There were other letters, ugly, angry screeds written by strongly opinionated people who felt the need to take pen to paper and blame the people of Bath for May 18, 1927.[10]

One writer peppered his missives with incoherent rants and biblical verses. Some letters came by mail; others were found in the street.[11]

"In every community there are unbalanced minds which need only some spectacular disaster, such as occurred at Bath . . . to set their deficient minds in a turmoil," wrote one newspaper editor. "It now develops that Kehoe himself became first a crank and then a maniac. People who show indications of even mild insanity should be reported to the proper authorities before some great damage is done."[12]

On another front, the Ku Klux Klan distributed a broadsheet, claiming that Kehoe's Catholic background was the root cause of his actions. The Klan, a relic of America's Reconstruction era past, was on the rise during the postwar era. The 1915 release of D. W. Griffiths's epic film *The Birth of a Nation,* coupled with the notorious Leo Frank case that same year (in which a Jewish pencil factory owner, found guilty in a trumped-up conviction for the rape and murder of a twelve-year-old girl, was lynched by an angry mob), gave new motivation to the once-dormant Klan. The great influx of immigrants; fear of blacks, Jews, and Catholics; and the rising menace of Bolsheviks in Russia fomented dissent in the form of men in white sheets. Klan membership is estimated to have been 4.5 million by 1924.[13] Its influence was formidable among movers and shakers; Hugo Black, a rising young Alabama politician—and later a U.S. Supreme Court justice—was a member.[14] There was a considerable Klan presence in Michigan as well; reportedly, Sheriff Fox was a Klansman.[15]

The pamphlet—of which five million copies of its "first edition" were allegedly printed—was typical propaganda, short on subtlety and long on fearmongering. Paragraph after paragraph detailed Kehoe's Catholicism in all its depravity. Numerous quotes were pulled from Catholic publications to prove the Klan's case against Kehoe. One citation, written by a priest in 1873, read, "The children of the Public Schools turn out to be horse thieves, scholastic counterfeiters and well versed in the schemes of deviltry. I frankly confess that Catholics stand before the country as the enemies of the Public Schools." Summing up its truth-challenged study of Catholicism and its influence on Kehoe, the anonymous Klan writer ended with a loaded rhetorical query: "Are [Kehoe's] actions in accordance with the dictates of the ecclesiastical voice? How long, O Lord, how long?"[16]

Blame could be found everywhere, it seemed, regardless of the facts.

◆ ◆ ◆

Senator Couzens, accompanied by Governor Green, toured the ruins on June 16; afterward they visited with children still hospitalized in Lansing.[17]

As a respected—and well-heeled—politician, Couzens's arrival had a second purpose. He would personally fund the rebuilding of the Bath Consolidated School.

Couzens's offer ended any discussion of what to do with the school property. Both he and the governor were in agreement: Bath Consolidated should be rebuilt on the same site. The following week, a telegram to the school board from Couzens's office solidified everything. "My views are the school be put in the same condition as before explosion," Couzens wrote. "Have asked Warren Holmes to get in touch with you at meeting tomorrow and report my views."

The Warren-Holmes-Powers Company, a Lansing architectural firm that created the original building's design, was well known to the school board. With the senator graciously offering to pay for the new facility— estimated to run anywhere between eighty and one hundred thousand dollars—the trustees were left with no other choice. Albert Detluff wired Senator Couzens's office. "We are pleased to accept your gracious offer to rebuild our school and accept same in behalf of the Bath Consolidated School district," he replied on behalf of the board. "Have asked Warren Holmes to confer with you."[18]

◆ ◆ ◆

The Bath Consolidated School bombing dominated newspaper headlines around the world on May 18 and 19. It was an unprecedented event, a mass murder of schoolchildren by one man, an act of sweeping horror. The kind of thing that sold newspapers with big, bold headlines heralding stories marked by fevered prose.

On May 20, everything changed.

That morning at 7:52 a.m., another Michigan-born man, the pilot Charles Lindbergh, pointed his small aircraft—dubbed *The Spirit of St. Louis*—to the eastern skies. Taking off from Roosevelt Field on Long Island, New York, Lindbergh headed toward France. In 1919, a wealthy hotelier, Raymond Orteig, had put up twenty-five thousand dollars as prize money for the first pilot to successfully make a solo flight between New York and Paris. Several internationally known flyboys died attempting to make the dangerous trip. Lindbergh, a relatively unknown barnstormer and mail pilot, was intent on winning the Orteig Prize.

Man and machine, daring the forces of nature, were attempting the impossible. It was a story rich with promise. Other news items fell to the wayside. Lindbergh captured the world's attention in a way no media darling had ever done before. His progress was breathlessly reported in extra editions of major and minor newspapers. When Lindbergh finally reached Paris, some 33 hours, 30 minutes, and 29.8 seconds after takeoff, people around the world hailed him as a hero.

The tragedy of a small Michigan town was barely worth a mention after that. If anything, it was generally relegated to back pages, perhaps taking up a column's worth of newsprint at best. Andrew Kehoe's bombing was old news, a curious story but not a gripping fact of everyday life to people outside of Bath.

As spring rolled into summer, the Bath Consolidated School bombing was completely out of the public spotlight. An earthquake in China killed two hundred thousand people on May 22. Lindbergh's triumphant return to the United States was heralded on June 15 with an extraordinary ticker tape parade down Fifth Avenue in New York. Throughout the summer, the fate of two anarchists, Nicola Sacco and Bartolomeo Vanzetti, was debated until the pair was executed on August 23.

What happened in Bath was old news to the rest of the world. But in local homes and hospitals, the aftermath was very much alive.

For two weeks, Dean Sweet lay comatose in the hospital. Doctors feared his chest wounds might kill the boy. There was grave concern that his heart would stop beating at any moment. Periodically they gave the unconscious child sips of whiskey to maintain a steady heart rhythm.[19]

The whiskey—illegal under the laws of Prohibition—did the trick. Dean pulled out of the coma. Yet for weeks on end he remained in danger. Sometimes his heartbeat was so intense that his bed would rattle and shake.

Dean remained in the hospital for several months. Periodically he had unwanted visitors, strangers come to stare, take photographs, and then disappear.

He felt like an animal in a zoo, unhappy at being caged and unable to change the situation on his own accord.[20]

Days after the bombing, doctors feared the number of dead would rise to fifty-one. Five children—Josephine England, Florence Hunter, Donald Huffman, Helen Komm, and Gail Stebleton—were on death watch. Their injuries were too severe; recovery seemed impossible.

The quintet proved to be fighters. They defied expectations and medical predictions. By summer's end, all five had been released from the hospital.[21]

Throughout the summer Willis Cressman's legs were sore. He figured it was from the jump he'd made from the roof to the ground when he escaped from the school.[22]

On July 14, Earl Proctor spent his thirteenth birthday lying in a hospital bed immobile. His badly broken legs were slowly healing; his left ankle now had a silver plate holding the bones together. The thighbone of his right leg was also broken. When he was found in the rubble, Earl's pants were gone, torn from his body in the explosion. Debris had ripped into his back, and his hips were in bad shape as a result. Additionally his head was sliced open in three places.[23] Although he was released after nine weeks, the severity of Earl's injuries put him back in the hospital now and then over the next year.[24]

Perry Hart's foot was in danger. After four months in the hospital, doctors were still uncertain about amputation. Infections and the looming possibility of gangrene were always close at hand. Whenever Perry got out of bed, the flesh around the drain tubes on his foot grew swollen

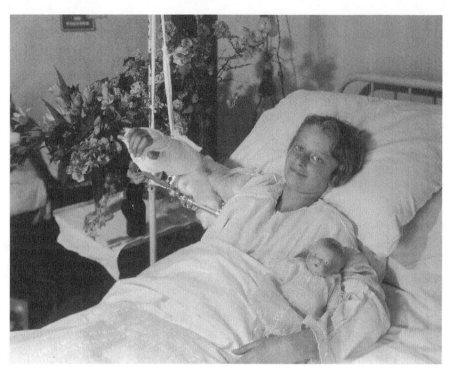

Fig. 16. Pauline Johns, age eleven. Her arm was broken in two places and the muscles torn. She was in the hospital for eight weeks. Her younger sister, Doris, was killed. *(Courtesy of the Bath School Museum.)*

from constant infection. Despite the physical and emotional pain he felt—his family had been hit hardest by the blast, after all, with his two sisters and one brother killed—he did not complain. One thing Perry did have in his favor was his overall health. He was a strapping teenager, strong and in good health. These factors, coupled with his stoic demeanor, went a long way toward his eventual recovery.[25]

Throughout the summer, a steady flow of outsiders filed past the ruined school and farm. They took loose bricks with them or scooped up small chunks of dirt from the Kehoe farm as souvenirs—of sorts—to remember their visits.

Monty Ellsworth was in prime position to benefit from the tourist trade. Living about a quarter of a mile from the Kehoe farm showed him that people wanted to take home a piece of Bath, some kind of keepsake or memento to mark their visits. There had to be something more tasteful than clods of dirt.

Fig. 17. "Tourists" combing through the destroyed Kehoe farm. *(Photograph by Fred A. Stevens.)*

Ellsworth's answer was a book that could be sold to passersby. "I have tried to tell every detail of the disaster that would be of interest to the reader," he wrote in the preface. "Everything in this book is the truth to the best of my ability."[26] The book was rife with errors, most notably stating that Kehoe was fourteen rather than forty when the family stove blasted his stepmother. Ellsworth was not a natural born writer, yet for the most part the booklet, titled simply *The Bath School Disaster* and bound in a plain brown cover, was composed with an understated eloquence. Ellsworth provided some background on the school, a sketchy biography of Kehoe, and a fairly accurate account of how the morning of May 18 unfolded. From friends in town, Ellsworth gathered photographs and biographical information on the victims and added small paragraphs with brief histories—including burial sites—of each person killed. He also reported on individual recoveries of the wounded. The book included a list of dead and wounded, organizations that provided aid, memorial poems, an eyewitness account written by a fifteen-year-old survivor, Martha Hintz, and a comprehensive index. Ellsworth paid for the booklet with personal funds and hired local boys to sell his work to the tourists. It was an easy product to move. The boys ran back and forth between Kehoe's farm and the schoolhouse peddling their wares, dropped the money off at Ellsworth's, collected their salaries, got more books, and went back to selling.[27]

◆ ◆ ◆

Doctors at the Saint Lawrence Hospital thought they were going to lose Beatrice Gibbs. The fourth grader was in terrible shape when she was brought in on May 18: both legs broken in two places with the right one badly sliced open, left arm with a shattered elbow and a bad break just above, another laceration on the back of her head, and cuts and bruises everywhere. Physicians rethought her treatment; standard care was not an option. The surface wounds must be carefully monitored, thus there could be no wrapping of Beatrice's broken bones in plaster casts. Instead she was nestled inside a complicated frame bed, her body suspended from ropes and held in place with thirty-five-pound lead weights. This took the pressure off her gashes while holding Beatrice's bones in place.

One day passed, then another. Beatrice hovered between life and death. On the fifth day, she came around. With so many children dead, Beatrice's battle back toward recovery was a welcome miracle. Gradually the weights were reduced and her bones and skin knitted back together. Eventually her doctors brought the balancing weights down to five pounds. What they could not do was alleviate Beatrice's crushing pain, an unending torture from within.

More surgery was required on August 22 to remove a splinter from her hip. Beatrice was too far gone, though; she died the next day. With her passing, the death toll from Kehoe's bombing numbered forty-five: thirty-eight children and five adults plus Andrew and Nellie Kehoe.[28]

Dean Sweet came home with strict orders not to move. Any strenuous activity—such as walking—could whip his heart into a frenzy. Doctors privately told his parents not to expect their son to live past his fifteenth birthday.

He longed to be outside. Dean wanted fresh air, to run and play like any other kid. Instead he was confined to the house, forced to sit day after day in a chair. Ava was by his side as Dean's activities turned girlish, threading beads and learning the art of crochet.

It was more than one boy could take. Rebellion had to come, even if it meant death.

As soon as he had a chance Dean sneaked outside, headed straight for the fields next to the house, and went for a walk. The fresh air felt good in his lungs, the sun warm on his skin, the earth firm beneath his feet.

When Willard Sweet saw his son outside, he panicked. "Dean," he pleaded, "please go back inside."

"No," Dean said. He'd had his taste of freedom. No one and no thing could bring him back into the house.

In 2001, when he was in his late eighties, Dean told a reporter that this moment of stubborn defiance forever crystallized in his mind as the day he finally started getting better.[29]

Galen Harte's mother couldn't bear to look at her son's pony; it was a constant reminder of the child she had lost in the explosion. Rather than keep the animal, she gave it to Carlton Hollister, Galen's best friend, asking him to watch the Shetland for a while.

Carlton stayed close to the pony throughout the summer. Galen's memory was close in mind every time Carlton saddled up for a ride. Taking care of his friend's beloved pony was both a privilege and a blessing, Carlton realized.

Still, he was filled with a youngster's wise sense of irony every time he sat in Galen's saddle. Because the boys had switched classrooms by chance on May 18, Carlton was alive and his friend was dead.[30]

Throughout the summer, Josephine Cushman cried. She cried to herself, she cried with friends, she cried with family. Her mother cried, too. Nellie Cushman would look at her daughter, unable to say anything but, "Oh, Josephine," then leave the room.

Any physical link to Ralph was painful. Nellie finally took all of his clothes and gave them to a family in need. There was one condition to this gift. Nellie didn't want any of the children receiving Ralph's things to wear them in front of Josephine.

But this, of course, was impossible. One day, as Josephine walked to town, she saw a boy wearing a tan shirt and tan pants. They looked familiar.

She realized the child was wearing Ralph's clothes.

It was a shock to the system. Josephine swallowed hard and kept walking. She didn't say a word to her parents, just as she didn't tell them about her back pains when Ralph's body was identified.

Her mother had tried to protect her by giving away Ralph's clothes, Josephine realized. And by not letting on about her encounter that day, she felt that she was protecting her parents as well.[31]

It should have been a nice day, a great day, when the Ringling Brothers, Barnum and Bailey Circus came to Lansing that summer. Lee Mast and his parents anticipated a day of clowns, wild animals, sideshows, and high-wire acts.

Instead the day took a bad turn. Winds blew into town, attacked the big top, and set its canvas flapping like a giant sail. Roustabouts furiously hammered down ropes, reinforcing the stakes that held the enormous tent.

There wasn't a spectator who wasn't scared during the fifteen minutes it took to stabilize the tent. Lee's fear felt different, though, he later said. After what he had been through in May, the loud flapping noises and surrounding human anxiety amplified the feelings induced by the nightmares he'd been having for a few weeks.[32]

Forced to lie in bed, Earl Proctor watched in anger as other children ran by his house. It seemed his boyhood had been stolen from him, just as his father had been three years earlier when he was killed in a car wreck. Pain and fear weighed heavily on Earl. He was terrified that he would be crippled for life.

On the day he went to be fitted for leg braces, he was slapped with new anxieties. The salesman looked over Earl and his widowed mother. In a harsh tone the clerk barked out, "Who's going to pay for them?"[33]

A six-year-old boy can comprehend the notion of death; understanding a loved one's passing is something else entirely. Billy Hall knew his older brother and sister, George and Willa, were gone, as he confided to his uncle, Andrew Green.

"Now I can have George's coveralls and tricycle because he ain't coming home any more," Billy told Uncle Andy. "My mother told me he wasn't."[34]

Measured in numbers, the loss of human lives—particularly those of children—is a stark equation of death. The fourth grade lost eight students killed and eleven injured out of twenty-one total. The fifth grade lost five students and eight injured out of twenty-four total. Twenty-eight children were enrolled in the sixth grade; twelve were killed and eleven injured. The highest death toll was in the school's third grade: ten of the sixteen students had died and three had been injured.[35]

Chapter 13

TULIPS

After the Columbine and Virginia Tech shootings in 1999 and 2007, re-spectively, shooting victims, families, other students, and school faculty and staff members were offered counseling, understandably and with compassion. They had lived through an inexplicable hell. Psychological help was a merciful balm.

On May 19, 1927, in Bath, people simply went back to work. Many of them had no choice. Crops needed tending; cows must be milked; other animals required daily care. Farm life does not allow for a day off re-gardless of the circumstances. Solace is found in quiet moments working the fields or at church on Sunday mornings.

Though all the victims were pulled from the ruins of the north wing, the debris remained. Throughout the summer volunteers worked hard removing rubble. Children pitched in, pulling nails out of broken tim-bers. Curious visitors, on day trips to see the remains, carted away bricks and other relics.

Many families stayed in Bath. It was their home. Others could not live with the memories lingering throughout the town. The glimpse of a child, a former playmate of a murdered son or daughter, was too much to bear. Wagons and trucks laden with furniture and families leaving

Fig. 18. Women and children removing nails from salvaged beams of the damaged building. *(Courtesy of the Bath School Museum.)*

town were common sights, though rarely discussed. One survivor observed that Bath "was almost a ghost town for many years."[1]

Cleanup work continued throughout the summer. It was a dirty, exhausting task, moving rubble for disposal while salvaging anything that could be used in rebuilding the school.

It was also dangerous work. Despite the hundreds of pounds of explosives removed in May, caution was paramount. No one wanted to take a chance on setting off any unexploded dynamite hidden beneath the rubble.

It was a smart move. On July 19, workers found amid the ruins a sack of dynamite and a kerosene-soaked rug. A ventilator was packed with mounds of small wood shavings, shoved inside for use as an accelerant.[2] One month later another cache of explosives was discovered. The well-wrapped bundle contained 244 sticks of dynamite, more than two hundred pounds' worth. It was carefully concealed beneath the first floor not far from the ruined north wing.[3]

There were no newspaper reporters on the scene when the children of Bath returned to school in the fall. For a village still in deep shock and mourning, this was a blessed relief.

With the school under repair, the children needed classrooms. The one-room schoolhouse model was not an option; children and their parents relied on a central location. The Lansing School Board generously offered "free of charge" education for the upcoming year, an offer that was eventually turned down. It was vital that Bath move forward. Although the school building was unusable for the time being, learning would continue.[4]

Downtown Bath became a campus of sorts. Students met on all three floors of the Community Hall where just a few months before some of their peers were laid out in a temporary morgue. Classes were held in the grocery store, drugstore, barbershop, firehouse, barns, houses, garages, and offices. With a little imagination and coordination, just about any space could be transformed into a classroom.

The annual return to school, however hodgepodge it was, represented newness, that wonderful feeling that returned every September. In Bath, the annual ritual held deeper significance. Friends were gone. Not quite 14 percent of the school population was killed on May 18.

Children who walked to school didn't always take a direct route to their new classrooms; many took out of the way jogs to avoid the ruins of Bath Consolidated. The wounds—some physical, many psychological—needed time to heal.

Willis Cressman's classes met in the grocery store. Getting to class was simple enough: enter the store, walk around the pickle barrels and rows of dry goods, take a seat, and begin learning. One windy day, in the middle of a lesson, the classroom door slammed shut. A loud *bang!* resounded off the walls like dynamite.

Cressman jumped out of his seat and instinctively ran for the door, pumping his legs furiously. He didn't know how he got out of the building, but somehow he was safe on the other side of the street.

He stopped, caught his breath, turned around, and saw that the store was still intact. Cressman's classmates swarmed the sidewalk. He realized later that when the noise of the door cracked through the air *everyone* had bolted.[5]

At the end of summer Josephine Cushman was sent to live with relatives in Holt, a town about twenty miles from Bath. Her parents felt it was best, thinking that a return to school would only remind Josephine of her losses on May 18.

Every Friday Josephine took the train from Holt to Bath to stay with her parents for the weekend; every Sunday she was put on the return train back to Holt.

It didn't sit well with her. Although she loved her cousins, Josephine wanted nothing more than to be back home permanently. She developed a terrible itch. Probably lice, the grownups deduced. A doctor checked but found no physical cause for her condition.

After six weeks of commuting back and forth, Josephine decided she'd had enough. She wasn't sure what she would tell her parents, though she knew she had to say something.

It came out unexpectedly, catching both Josephine and her parents by surprise. "You know, I'm not going back there!" she boldly declared one Sunday. Immediately, she felt, it was the wrong thing to say, but Nellie and Albert remained silent. Josephine's weekly trips between Holt and Bath came to a sudden end.

Still, her mother was nervous about letting Josephine return to school. It didn't matter that classes were now held in buildings throughout the downtown area; as far as Nellie Cushman was concerned, Josephine wasn't going back to the Bath Consolidated School.

To Josephine this was just as bad as living in Holt. The house seemed empty without Ralph. She needed to be with her classmates.

Although the setting of the Bath school had changed, its essence remained the same. There still were school parties for the children, still a sense of normalcy in the wake of destruction.

An old-fashioned wienie roast proved to be Josephine's salvation. Gordon Hollister, who, like Josephine, was fourteen years old, asked her to be his date. With her parents' permission, she was allowed to attend. It was exactly what she needed. Being with old friends, having the chance to be a regular teenager once more, gave her a fresh outlook on life. When Josephine came home that evening, Albert and Nellie could see the joy on their daughter's face.

"Did you have a good time?" her mother asked.

"The best time I've had in a long time," Josephine said. "It was so much fun being with all those kids."

After Sunday dinner the next evening, Albert and Nellie sat down with their daughter. "Josephine," Nellie said, "would you like to go back to school?"

"Oh, yes!" she said, her voice barely audible. "I would love it."

"Okay," said Nellie. "Get your things ready and you can go back."

Josephine felt breathless, as if a terrible burden had been lifted from her.[6]

The cornerstone of the new school was put in place on November 1, 1927, nearly six months after the bombing. A brief ceremony marked the occasion with Superintendent Brandt providing a few words along with Dean Phelan of Michigan State College and Mattie Smith, the county school commissioner.[7]

Come May 1928 commencement exercises were held as scheduled. Ten members of the class, five women and five men, posed for a picture with Superintendent Brandt. In their portrait, the graduates—most of whom had been injured, lost loved ones, or both—looked at the camera with somber expressions.[8]

The idea of a memorial park was scrapped, but a collective yearning for something to honor the dead remained. "Any memorial that is erected to the martyred children in Bath may reach higher than the tower of Babel, yet be diminished by contrast with the black pillar of anguish that will be in the breasts and brains of their parents when they gaze dim-eyed at man's effort to close an incident tenderly—a tiny hillock blanketed with grass, as with a benediction," wrote Frank Pritchard of the *Lansing State Journal*.

Exactly what could be deemed a fitting tribute was a point of contention. When the parade of tourists faded, when the children went back to school, when news would again be dominated by farming and commerce, when the Community Hall was again a place for meetings and entertainment, when Bath returned to normal—or at least a shadow of normal—this memorial must be something for future generations to comprehend, a mark on the world that spoke of the unbearable grief that ensued when thirty-eight children and five adults (plus two others) were wiped out.[9]

On August 18, 1928, another ceremony took place, dedicating the new educational facility, renamed the James Couzens Agricultural School after its benefactor. Ultimately the rebuilding cost Senator Couzens seventy-five thousand dollars. One of the speakers was L. L. Tyler, the principal of the old Bath High School some forty years earlier and now a professor at Alma College, located fifty miles north of Lansing.

A silent greeter stood in the school's central lobby, a bronze statue of a ten-year-old girl holding a cat under her right arm. This sculpture, created by Carleton Angell of the University of Michigan, was funded by schoolchildren throughout the state at the suggestion of Professor Tyler. Tyler had proposed that students from every school in Michigan donate a few pennies for a memorial honoring their fallen peers. It was an inspired move. Coins arrived in droves from all of Michigan's five hundred school districts.[10] (Rumors abounded through the years that the statue's metal was copper, melted down and recast from the thousands of pennies that paid for its creation.)

The figure, titled simply "Girl with a Cat," did not speak to the tragedy. Rather it represented all children, the face of the future, a rebirth of hope, the powerful strength of human resilience.

◆ ◆ ◆

The Kehoe property reverted back to the Price family. Unable to face the shadow on that land, they donated the grounds to Sisters of Mercy, the Catholic order that oversaw the Saint Lawrence Hospital.

Nothing was done with the property. In the late 1930s, it was bought by Otis Van Ostran. Everyone told the new owner he was a fool for buying such tainted ground. Didn't he know the place was a potential minefield still packed with buried dynamite? One never knew if Kehoe had planted explosives in the ground in one last effort to wreak revenge on Bath. Yet Van Ostran was determined; after all, it made no sense to let good soil go to waste.

The first time he plowed, Van Ostran later told people, he felt his heart in his throat.[11]

The skeletal brick traces of what was once a farmhouse remained standing throughout the seasons for years on end, crumbling, growing more silent over time.[12]

◆ ◆ ◆

A powerful rainstorm struck Bath on June 1, 1943. The dark clouds grew furious, firing rain and lightning on the town. Thunder exploded like dynamite. The storm boiled over, erupting into a twister. Its winds turned barns into piles of sticks. Animals were haphazardly picked up and dropped across farmlands.[13]

Ava Sweet Nelson took her two children to the cellar for safety. The thunder was deafening. For a moment, it seemed like she was back in sixth grade with piles of bricks falling around her as the explosion racked the school.

It took years for Ava's daughter Alice to understand why her mother became hysterical during the storm.[14]

◆ ◆ ◆

One of the duties of the company nurse at the REO Motor Car factory in Lansing was to note the physical appearance of workers lest they try to blame their employer for past injuries. On this day, a worker, his face lined with old scars, came into her office.

She tried not to stare but managed to steal a few glances. The worker caught her furtive looks and started to explain. Almost twenty years ago when he was a kid, he'd attended a rural school where something terrible happened. "You would not know about it," he told her. "It was a small town you never heard of. A crazy man who worked as our janitor one day blew up the school, his house with his wife in it and his farm buildings, cattle, horses . . . and finally himself."

He did not know the company nurse had formerly worked at Sparrow Hospital. She was there on May 18, 1927. She'd borne witness to the bombing, to the chaos. She'd tended to the horror of the wounded children.

"I know," she told the man.[15]

◆ ◆ ◆

In one home, a closet remained padlocked year after year, growing dusty and seemingly unused. Stored within was the clothing of a child who died on May 18, 1927. The victim's mother couldn't bear to part with her son's clothing, the last vestige of the boy's brief time on Earth.[16]

Throughout his life, Dean Sweet's head was marked with a jagged purple scar, a permanent reminder of the debris that had cracked his skull. Periodically his skin would become pockmarked with small bumps, remnants of wood particles still trapped within his body trying to work their way out.[17]

Earl Proctor's fears of disability and poverty never amounted to much. He had a long career in the insurance industry before his retirement. He made his home in the house once owned by his grandparents, the place where he spent so many hours recovering after the bombing.

Yet he always limped on the left side and in his later years relied on a walker. He was unable to stand straight on his left ankle, which remained forever bent at an odd angle.[18]

During World War II, Florence Hart's son Neal fought in the South Pacific. She couldn't help but worry; her older boy Robert, gone some eighteen years now, was always close to Florence's heart. She didn't want another child to perish by violence. "I don't know if I can stand losing another son," she often told people.

On one rare occasion, Neal called home, spending a few precious minutes speaking with his mother from overseas

The connection sounded tinny and crackly at its best. "He's calling from so far away," Florence thought. "This must be what a phone call from Heaven must sound like. This is what it would be like to talk to Robert if he could call me."[19]

The vanquishing of his ten-year-old daughter Elizabeth haunted Roscoe Witchell throughout the years. When he was in his early sixties, Witchell suffered a minor stroke. During his rehabilitation, therapists tried to help him relearn how to write his name. It was a fruitless endeavor. Every time he took pen to paper, Roscoe would write "Elizabeth."[20]

In the 1960s and 1970s there were periodic bomb threats made on the Couzens School. These were forewarnings not taken lightly. Children were evacuated, sent home on school buses, and not allowed to return until the school was deemed safe.

Julie Hudnut was on the young side of her first grade class in 1968. She'd started school at five years old, a year sooner than her classmates. Regardless of her age, she thought school was fascinating with so much to see and do and learn. The teacher, Mrs. Bethel Pierce, was a sweet woman and wonderful instructor who cared deeply about her students. Julie felt great affection for Mrs. Pierce, though she couldn't help but notice her teacher was older than most of the other faculty.

On one memorable day, the shrill clang of the alarm bell sounded throughout the Couzens School. Mrs. Pierce, asked the class to get up, please walk outside and stay in single file. Her students did as they were told, following their teacher down the hall to the doors. As she marched with her class, Julie heard two words being whispered throughout the hallway.

"Bomb threat."

Mrs. Pierce led the students to what was referred to as "the safe spot," a small field at the edge of the school property. Standing quietly with her classmates, Julie was stunned to see tears running down her teacher's cheeks. Although Mrs. Pierce remained in charge, not wavering in her duty to the children, Julie knew her teacher was going through something terrible. Through her tears, Mrs. Pierce's face had a haunted quality. Was it something about this moment, those words *bomb threat?*

Mrs. Pierce never told her students why she cried that day.

When Mrs. Pierce died on March 19, 2007, Julie fondly recalled her teacher. As she read Mrs. Pierce's obituary, a sentence leaped out.

Mrs. Pierce—formerly Bethel Tihart—was one of the children who survived Kehoe's bombing.[21]

Each time a bomb threat was made, Bath's volunteer firemen would go through the school to make sure all was safe. Each time it happened, the threat turned out to be nothing—just the work of pranksters with a penchant for scraping Bath's psychic wounds.

Wayne Loomis, a member of the volunteer firefighters, was well suited for inspecting the school whenever a threat was made: he worked in construction, knew how buildings were put together and where potential weaknesses might be found. He became an old hand at this sobering work. Six times he went out on such calls and six times found no bombs.

Though not a native of Bath, Loomis had family ties to the 1927 bombing. His mother-in-law, Ava Sweet Nelson, and her brother Dean were both survivors. One man he worked with had lost a child in the blast.

Whenever there was a bomb threat at the school, Loomis would crawl into the dark crevices of the building, carefully combing the floors, walls, and ceilings inch by inch. The beam of his flashlight would bounce around these tight spaces. In the darkness, bits and pieces of the past were illuminated. Loomis often saw scars in the building rafters where the original ceiling had been knocked loose. And when he went below into the depths of the basement, Loomis looked on aging patches that hid holes made by dynamite.[22]

◆ ◆ ◆

Over the years, the remains of the old farmhouse could still be seen on the former Kehoe land. The property regained its status as good growing soil. Ownership changed hands a few times, but those old bricks lingered

Fig. 19. Remnants of the Kehoe farm stood for several generations.
(Courtesy of the Bath School Museum.)

on. Weeds and bushes shrouded this vestige. For years parents warned youngsters to stay away lest they accidentally set off an old cache of dynamite. Of course, kids being kids, such warnings went unheeded. The wreckage turned into a taboo playground, but no one was ever blown to kingdom come.

And then one day the bricks were gone. The last traces of Kehoe had quietly been scrubbed from the Bath landscape.[23]

The post–World War II era was marked by remarkable growth in population and technology, two shifts that were reflected in school systems throughout the country. Bath was no exception. The James Couzens Agricultural School no longer met all of the community's educational needs. An elementary school was built in 1953, followed in 1961 by a second building. Both were across the road from the old Couzens School.[24]

In the late 1960s it was clear that the James Couzens School had outlived its usefulness. It was a shell of its former self, a worn and tattered structure no longer able to evolve with the times and plagued by a withering infrastructure. A 1967 study by experts at Michigan State University recommended "abandonment at the earliest opportunity."[25] School board members and administrators struggled over a solution. But change was inevitable. Couzens closed its doors in 1975, replaced by a modern high school at another location.[26]

Now stuck with an empty building, the school board contracted with a wrecking company to tear down the shuttered facility. Razing what was left of James Couzens Agricultural School was not a popular idea with some Bath residents. It was almost like tearing down a sacred tabernacle. The old building still had some life in it, they insisted. It could be turned into a library or retirement housing for senior citizens.[27]

Sentiment was overruled. On May 18, 1975, Julie Hudnut, now a pretty thirteen year old, sat quietly with her seventh grade classmates in the Bath Middle School. She looked out the window, gazing at the old Couzens School. An enormous wrecking ball, resembling a mechanical dinosaur about to devour its prey, loomed next to the building.

Mr. Vandyke, the school principal, asked for a few minutes of silence for those killed in the 1927 bombings, timing his announcement to the moment of the first explosion. Julie bowed her head. She expected the silent meditation to come and go and inevitably be pocketed with giggles and whispers.

She closed her eyes, thinking hard about the children of 1927. The silence went on far longer than she expected. Not a person moved, not a laugh or muffled voice broke through the solemnity. "It's so quiet you could hear a pin drop," she thought.

Julie shivered a little as a strange chill coursed through her body. The silence was eerie, a void of sound, a profound contrast to the chaotic pandemonium of 1927.

She raised her head, then looked out the window. Julie saw the sun glinting off the wrecking ball across the street. It took a hard swing, signaling once more the destruction of the school. Debris crashed to the ground as the first section scheduled for razing, the north wing of the building, was knocked down.

Again Julie shivered. Kehoe's dynamite had destroyed the north wing of the Bath Consolidated School on this same day at almost the same time.[28]

After it was torn down, the school remains were scattered. The hole that once was the basement was filled in and covered with fresh sod. Some residents took bricks as precious talismans of the past. Other debris was dumped in a nearby swamp. The marshy land later became a housing development.[29]

"Girl with a Cat" was relocated to the Bath High School foyer. The white cupola, which originally crowned the Bath Consolidated School, was saved.

What remained of the old school grounds was still sacred within the community. The area was landscaped, outfitted with benches, and rededicated as the James J. Couzens Memorial Park. On the edge of the park stood the Bath Methodist Church, essentially the same as when the class of 1927 planned to use it for its commencement. Just outside the sanctuary was a plaque with the names of all who died in the blast.

The old cupola was placed in the center of the park, close to the spot where it originally stood.

May 21, 1977, was graduation day at the high school. The event sparked renewal for some former students. During the commencement diplomas were given to alumni from the class of 1927.

In the five decades since the bombing, there was no reunion for the class of 1927. Five graduates had passed away; another member now lived in Alaska. Those who remained in Bath wore the traditional mortarboard and graduation gown. James Hixson, superintendent for the Bath School District, signed diplomas.[30]

The graduates—now in their late sixties—posed for a class portrait. Smiles abounded on the faces of the six women and three men.[31]

Three days earlier, on Wednesday, May 18—the same day and date as in 1927—there was another ceremony. A bronze plaque, unveiled in Couzens Park, noted the history of the site from its first school building in 1873 to the opening of Bath Consolidated School, Senator Couzens's donation funding the rebuilding in 1928, and the 1975 school board decision to tear down the outdated building.

The third paragraph of the plaque is simple and direct. "May 18, 1927, a disaster struck this community and the school was demolished by dynamite perpetrated by Andrew P. Kehoe, killing 45 and injuring 58 children and adults."[32]

The afternoon was solemn yet uplifting. The school band and community chorus provided music, the local Cub Scout pack raised the American flag, and a National Guard firing squad shot off a salute after each victim's name was read aloud; when the 21 gun salute ended, the traditional "Taps" was played. State and local politicians were present, and Superintendent Hixson provided a few words honoring the moment.

Three witnesses of the bombing were also present. Floyd Huggett, the school principal in 1927, and Nina Matson Fair, one of the teachers, were among the guests. Fondly remembered as Miss Matson by her students, Fair unveiled the monument that afternoon. She was asked to say a few words; fearing she might break down, Fair asked her son-in-law to speak on her behalf.[33]

Also in the audience was Ethel Huyck Saur, Emory Huyck's widow.[34]

Memories held firm throughout the decades, and loved ones lost to terror were never far away. After fifty years, a public memorial was finally dedicated on behalf of the dead.

◆ ◆ ◆

In March 1985, a permanent exhibit was installed at the middle school. Dubbed the Bath School Museum, this facility gives visitors a glimpse of the past with artifacts from the old one-room schoolhouses, mementos from graduating classes, an antique school desk complete with an inkwell holder, and educational tools such as old *Dick and Jane* books.

Naturally, the museum is dominated by the reminders of May 18, 1927. The flag that flew at the school that morning. A clock, hands frozen at the exact time the dynamite went off. An autograph book belonging to one of the victims. A chair picked up and taken home by a frightened kindergartner. Newspaper stories and memoirs of survivors are mounted on the wall. Photographs of the ruined north wing, the bushel baskets of dynamite, the remnants of Kehoe's truck. A picture of Andrew and Nellie Kehoe, sitting in their living room, looking as content as any farm couple.

In a corner, protected by an acrylic case, is the bronze statue "Girl with a Cat." A plaque explains its significance.

A large photograph of Superintendent Huyck hangs over the entrance. There is a hint of a smile within his no-nonsense demeanor.

He is a man looking with pride over his school.

◆ ◆ ◆

Florence Hart checked into the hospital in early January of 1988 for a blood transfusion. Doctors insisted she stay overnight, which didn't set

Fig. 20. Superintendent Emory E. Huyck. *(Courtesy of the Bath School Museum.)*

too well with Florence. She knew she was at the end of her life and was frustrated over her declining health. Most of her friends and so many loved ones were gone. But she was not alone; her children and grandchildren were a great comfort.

Still, Florence knew she was missing something. Only death could provide the one thing she really wanted.

Patti Seehase, Florence's granddaughter, sat at the bedside. The two shared a deep affection; it would be hard for Patti when the inevitable came for her grandmother.

But Florence was ready to go. She was practically bursting with anticipation. "You know, Patti," she said, "I'm getting so excited to see Robert. I love all of you kids, don't get me wrong. But I'm so excited to see Robert again I can hardly stand it. I don't know what the Lord is keeping me here for now."

A few days later, Florence slipped into a coma. She died six weeks later on February 16, just ten days shy of her ninety-fourth birthday. Florence took with her a deep, abiding faith in God, love of family, and the precious thought that after more than sixty years apart she would reunite with her son.[35]

◆ ◆ ◆

Shortly before 9:00 a.m. on April 19, 1995, Timothy McVeigh, a disillusioned Gulf War veteran parked his rented truck in front of the Alfred P. Murrah Federal Building in Oklahoma City. The vehicle was loaded with nearly five thousand pounds of the agricultural fertilizer ammonium nitrate mixed with nitromethane, a highly explosive fuel used in drag racers and rockets. McVeigh calmly ignited a timed fuse inside the truck, then quickly exited the area.

At 9:02 a.m., McVeigh's crude bomb went off. It ripped open the front of the Murrah Building, ultimately killing 168 people and injuring about 850 others. Nineteen of the dead were children, killed in the day care center located on the ground floor of the facility. It took hours to save survivors caught in the debris.

As she watched the story unfold on television, Ava Sweet Nelson, now living in Florida, flashed back to another spring day when she was trapped in rubble for hours, screaming and praying for rescuers.

She cried all that day for the victims. Ava knew exactly how they felt.[36]

Television news, searching for meaning and looking for answers, descended on Bath. In the wake of Oklahoma City, the story of Andrew Kehoe and the Bath Consolidated School was retold to a nation that had long forgotten about the bombing.

The NBC program *Dateline* titled its piece "Blood Bath."

◆ ◆ ◆

In another dedication ceremony, held on May 18, 1992, the sixty-fifth anniversary of the bombing, Couzens Park was officially dedicated as a Michigan Historic Site with a marker installed detailing the location's significance.

For the seventy-fifth commemoration in 2002, the Bath Area Jaycees laid out a brick walkway encircling the cupola. Each victim's name was memorialized within the path. A boulder, donated by Bath Township, was also installed that day. The giant stone was outfitted with a plaque listing most of those killed in the bombing. Two names were omitted: Andrew and Nellie Kehoe.[37]

◆ ◆ ◆

Jennie Hanson, who taught art at Bath Middle School in 1998, was told her eighth-grade students were known troublemakers. It was no exaggeration. She watched helplessly as kids picked fights or split into cliques.

There had to be something to unite the kids. Hanson was determined to bring the disruptive bunch together as one, using self-expression as the conduit.

She found inspiration in the past, conceiving a new sculpture for the Bath School Museum. Her students would create the piece, a memorial to their 1927 peers.

Hanson sketched her idea, a willow tree with ceramic tiles on its branches to represent the bombing victims. Above her drawing, she drafted an artistic statement.

> A tree shape symbolic of growth and life. A willow to show sorrow for those who died or were injured. Bright tiles for hope. The slight movement of the tiles in a breeze shows life.

The eighth graders each picked a name, a life to portray in clay and glaze. They talked to relatives and friends, looked at Monty Ellsworth's book, and read other accounts of the tragedy, then began to work. Each tile reflected something important about the person it symbolized.

The "Tree of Life" sculpture transformed the class. Fights were replaced with compassion. When Hanson read Hazel Weatherby's story to her students, she found herself choked with emotion. The children nestled in Weatherby's arms could easily be any of the kids in her classroom. Hanson could not hold back her tears.

The sculpture brought Hanson and her students closer to each other. A group of kids, written off as troublemakers, were united through their peers of 1927.

"I thought [the project] was going to be dumb," one student wrote when it was complete. Rather, she found new ideas within herself. "I learned more than just how to play with clay but how to deal with the sad stuff."[38]

❖ ❖ ❖

The Kehoe property changed hands a few times, though sometimes it was difficult to sell the land. Stories persisted through the years that somewhere beneath the soil Kehoe had buried secret dynamite caches. Few people wanted to chance stumbling on this potentially deadly inheritance.[39]

Beneath the area where the farmhouse once stood there ran a natural waterway some seven feet below the surface. When Neil Curtis, who acquired the land in the late 1990s, decided to access this resource he hired a contractor to do the digging. Curtis watched the process standing a half mile from what could be ground zero. No unexploded dynamite surfaced.

Curtis sometimes found old bricks, the remnants of Kehoe's three-story home, studding his fields. He dumped the useless relics unceremoniously into a ditch along Clark Road.[40]

◆ ◆ ◆

Elton McConnell, a former Michigander, who retired to Oregon, often told stories about what he saw on May 18. In 1927 he was a mechanic at the State Garage, an automobile repair shop for government employees. On that morning, he heard an explosion in the distance, went outside, and could see a pillar of smoke rising in the northeast. When the news broke, he raced to Bath; he had relatives who attended the school, and McConnell wanted to do what he could. He always described the scene as "a bloody mess."

Over the years McConnell would tell others how he remembered Kehoe driving up. There was a look of ghastly horror on the man's face. Next, McConnell recalled, Kehoe said something like, "Oh my God, it was supposed to go off last night!" In this scenario, Kehoe would have blown up the school during a Parent-Teacher Association meeting held on the night of May 17.[41]

His memories echo those of Sidney J. Howell, who seemingly martyred himself defending Kehoe. Although Kehoe surely intended the explosion to unfold almost exactly as it did, there is no surprise in false memories like McConnell's or Kehoe defenders like Sydney Howell. Despite the bombing of the Bath Consolidated School; despite Brenda Ann Spencer picking off students with her rifle at the Cleveland Elementary School in San Diego on January 29, 1979 (her reasoning, "I don't like Mondays," inspired a popular song by the Irish rock group The Boomtown Rats); despite Patrick Purdy's murder-suicide, killing five children and himself on January 17, 1989, at an elementary school—also named Cleveland—in Stockton, California; despite Laurie Dann's mad day on May 20, 1988 (71 years and 2 days after Kehoe's bombing), when she sent poisoned beverages to several Northwestern University fraternity houses, set off an incendiary device at one suburban Chicago elementary school, then stormed another where she killed one child, wounded several others, fled, forced her way into a nearby home, took refuge in an upstairs bedroom, stuck a gun in her mouth and fired; despite Barry

Loukaitis's murders on February 2, 1996, at the Frontier Junior High School in Moses Lake, Washington, where, clad in gunslinger garb and outfitted with two handguns, a rifle, and eighty rounds of ammunition, Loukaitis blasted away two children and a teacher; despite the April 20, 1999, rampage of Dylan Klebold and Eric Harris who, armed with an Intratec TEC–DC9, a Hi-Point 995 carbine, a Savage 67H pump-action shotgun, and a Stevens 311D double-barreled sawed-off shotgun, went on a bloody rampage, exploding one crude bomb (other explosive devices failed to go off) and shooting round after round at their high school in Columbine, Colorado, killing twelve students, one teacher and then each other; despite other such massacres throughout the United States, Canada, Denmark, Finland, Germany, and several Asian countries, it's hard to imagine human beings committing mass murder within the haven of a school, a place where children are supposed to be safe from harm.[42]

What little exists of Andrew and Nellie Kehoe's earthly goods gather dust in the Michigan Historical Museum: Kehoe's broken and battered watch, his driver's license, and Nellie's silverware. The remains of his truck were donated to a scrap drive during World War II.[43]

Kehoe's burial site remains unmarked but not alone. It is no small irony that years after his suicide, a child was buried next to Andrew Kehoe's grave.[44]

◆ ◆ ◆

Bath, Michigan. Friday May 18, 2007

The morning of May 18 was clean and clear, sun shining bright. A perfect spring day in Michigan.

Eighty years had passed since the day of destruction. Today Bath radiated normalcy, everyday routines of the small-town Midwest. Morning went by, as so many do, turning into a beautiful afternoon. Kids ached from sitting at their school desks. It was too nice a day to be inside.

Couzens Park was quiet but not without a certain ambience. Subtle memorials were brought to the greens, as remembrances of the 1927 devastation and death. Strewn here and there across the park were single flowers, a colorful tribute to young lives forever stilled. A cluster of flowers gently blanketed the brick pathway of names around the cupola.

All through the day a smattering of people came to the park to pay their respects and bear witness. Parents with children—many the ages of bombing victims—showed a new generation the memorials and retold the story.

That afternoon Nancy Welch Spagnulo, a longtime Bath resident, came to the cupola with a homemade wreath. She wasn't an old-timer in town. Her family had only been there since 1950, a relatively short span in the deeply rooted generations of townspeople. Yet the bombing was as close to her as anyone who'd grown up in Bath, a presence that was always near. Attending the old Couzens Agricultural School was a strange experience for her; she always felt as though she was awash in memory. Her family's house also carried a reminder of the day. Built in 1910, the home bore a crack at the top, unrepaired since it was ripped asunder eighty years before.

Spagnulo's wreath was decorated with herbs and flowers. Mint was for innocence. Rosemary for remembrance. And pansies for the children.[45]

The wreath was carefully hung on the front of the cupola.

◆ ◆ ◆

Over on Clark Road, the land that had once been the Kehoe farm was also quiet. The wind blew lightly across freshly plowed fields.

In the sky a lone hawk swooped through the air, scouting for prey. It rose swiftly, then dropped into a sudden dive. The hawk seemed to hover for a moment, then changed course and disappeared into the woods on the edge of the land.

◆ ◆ ◆

Josephine Cushman Vail was a little disappointed that morning. Mother's Day had just passed, and florists throughout the county were fresh out of red tulips. She made do with the best substitute she could find, a bouquet of orange roses.

Her granddaughter, Heather Chadwick, picked Josephine up for the drive to Pleasant Hill Cemetery. Not much was said along the way; Josephine was lost in her thoughts. The week had been a little hectic in Bath, what with newspapers and television stations coming in and out for a quick story on the eightieth anniversary. In the wake of Virginia Tech, it seemed the story had more relevance to readers and viewers this year.

Josephine was worried of late. Just shy of ninety-four, she was still a feisty woman in love with life and all it had given her. She had been making this annual May pilgrimage for decades. Josephine knew that it would eventually come to an end. Would Ralphie always get his red tulips?[46]

Don't worry, Heather assured her. Bringing Ralph tulips every May 18 was a deeply ingrained family tradition, one that would continue for years to come. He's part of me, part of my family, she told her grandmother.

Heather turned the car into the cemetery, slowly driving to the Cushman family plot. She helped her grandmother from the car for the short walk to Ralph's resting place.[47]

Slowly, with purpose, Josephine knelt by the headstone. "Ralphie, I'm here again," she whispered. She placed the roses next to his grave. For a moment, it was just the two of them. Josephine murmured a few words, an intimacy shared between sister and brother. She kissed her fingertips lightly, then touched them to Ralph's name.[48]

Overhead, the sweet song of spring birds drifted in the air.

VICTIMS' NAMES

THE DEAD

Bauerle, Arnold Victor, 8
Bergan, Henry, 14
Bergan, Herman, 11
Bromund, Robert, 12
Bromund, Emilie, 11
Burnett, Floyd Edwin, 11

Chapman, Russell, 8
Clayton, Cleo, 8
Cochran, Robert, 8
Cushman, Ralph Albert, 7

Ewing, Earl Edwin, 11

Foote, Katherine Onalee, 10 (died nine days before her tenth birthday, born May 29, 1917)

Fritz, Margory, 11

Geisenhaver, Carlyle Walter, 9
Gibbs, Beatrice, 10 (died August 23)

Hall, George, Jr., 10
Hall, Willa Marie, 12
Hart, Iola Irene, 12 (died one month short of her thirteenth birthday, born June 19, 1914)
Hart, Percy Eugene, 11
Hart, Vivian Oletta, 9
Harte, Blanche Elizabeth, teacher
Harte, Galen Lyle, 12
Harte, LaVere Robert, 9
Harte, Stanley Horace, 12
Hoppener, Francis Otto, 13

Hunter, Cecial Lorn, 13
Huyck, Emory E., superintendent

Johns, Doris Elaine, 7

Kehoe, Andrew P.
Kehoe, Nellie

McFarren, Clarence Wendell, 13
McFarren, Nelson
McDonald, Thelma Irene, 7
Medcoff, J. Emerson, 9

Nickols, Emma Amelia, 13

Richardson, Richard Dibble, 12
Robb, Elsie Mildred, 12

Shirts, Pauline Mae, 9 (died one day before her ninth birthday, born May 19, 1916)
Smith, Glenn O., postmaster

Weatherby, Hazel Iva, teacher
Witchell, Elizabeth Jane, 10
Witchell, Lucile June, 9
Woodman, Harold LeMoyne, 8

Zimmerman, George Orval, 10
Zimmerman, Lloyd, 12

THE INJURED

Babcock, Lloyd
Babcock, Norris
Babcock, Vera
Barnes, Ruth M.
Braska, Anna

Chapman, Earl

Delau, Arthur
Delau, Ida
Detluff, Ida
Dolton, Adabelle

Eschtruth, Iva
Eschtruth, Marian
Eschtruth, Raymond
England, Josephine

Foster, James
Frederick, Aletha
Fritz, Mr. F. M.
Fulton, Dorothy

Geisenhaver, Kenneth
Gubbins, Eva, teacher
Gutekunst, Leona, teacher

Hart, Elva
Hart, Perry
Hobert, Helen E.
Hobert, Ralph R.
Hollister, Carlton F.
Huffman, Donald J.
Huffman, June Rose
Hunter, Florence Edith

King, Lester
Komm, Florence
Komm, Helen

Mast, Lee Henry
Matson, Nina, teacher
McCoy, Pauline Mae
McCoy, Willis
McKenzie, Harold
Medcoff, Thelma

Nickols, Ottelia
Nickols, Ruth

Perrone, Mrs. J.
Proctor, Earl Fred
Proctor, Ralph Edmund

Reasoner, Lee
Reed, Lillian M.

Richardson, Martha Harriette
Richardson, Virginia Blanche
Riker, Oral
Rounds, Jack

Sage, Norman
Seeley, Ivan Freemont
Stebleton, Gail Edmund
Stivaviske, Steve
Stolls, Lester
Sweet, Ava Thelma
Sweet, Dean

Wilson, Ardis
Witchell, Kenneth

Zavistoski, Cecelia

ACKNOWLEDGMENTS

When I initially learned about the Bath School bombing, it seemed like a great tale for any author. My first visit to Pleasant Hill Cemetery profoundly changed that perception. This was a tragic reality punctuated by the graves of so many children. I am humbled to chronicle the tragedy of May 18, 1927, and there are so many people to thank for helping me on this journey.

First are the people of Bath, who welcomed a stranger and trusted me with their heartbreak. Foremost is my angel, Michelle Allen, who not only chased down every obscure and time-consuming request I made, she also fed me and bought me apple cider. Michelle, they don't make them better than you. This book simply would not have seen the light of day without your grace and hard work. I'm lucky to have you as a friend. The Bath School Museum Committee provided great support throughout; without the generous work of Elaine Barnard, James W. Hixson, Dean Sweet, Jr., and so many others this book just would not be the same. Gene Wilkins spent many hours sharing information and encouragement. Julie Teed is a great resource and a greater friend. Ronald D. Bauerle, 1977 Bath High School graduate, grandnephew of victim Arnold Bauerle, and creator of the Bath School Disaster Web site

(http://freepages.history.rootsweb.ancestry.com/~bauerle/disaster
.htm) provided invaluable information. James Daggy is another great
Web chronicler of the tragedy and gave me great help with his "Information about the Bath School Disaster" (http://daggy.name/tbsd).
Thanks also to Heather Chadwick, Dr. R. G. Curtis, Roger Friend, Alice
and Wayne Loomis, George Edward McConnell, John McGonigal, Florence Lowe Platt, and Patti Seehase.

Many of the photographs for this book were provided by the Bath
School Museum. I am also indebted to two others who generously shared
their family pictures: Timothy Howery; and Kent Curtis for photographs
taken by Fred A. Stevens (1891–1978) of Perry, Michigan.

My agent, Barbara Braun, who understood the importance of this
book far more than I did.

The good people at the University of Michigan Press: Ellen McCarthy,
Mary Erwin, Marcia LaBrenz, Scott Ham, and all their crew.

Alan Jacobson for legal advice and all-around menschhood. I miss
you every day.

David Votta of the Capital Area District Library in Lansing for an-
swering so many questions and tracking down article after article whenever I asked. Librarians of your caliber must be praised far and wide;
people like you are the reason I'm such a library geek.

Matt Martyn and Ahptic Film & Digital of Lansing for their generous
support and sharing of information.

Hank Ellison (plus Rose and Sarah and Sean!) and Tom VanSwol for
their expertise on technical issues.

Dana Lewandowski, who eloquently showed me the modern face of
school tragedy.

For advice, support, and suggestions: Rick Kogan, friend and mentor;
Randy Albers, teacher extraordinaire, and everyone at the Columbia
College Fiction Department; Jay Bonansinga; Josh Culley-Foster of the
Columbia College Alumni Office; Laura M. MacDonald; and Fern
Schumer. Thanks to a pair of wonderful scribes in their own right, Leigh
Anna Harken and Bethany Francisco, who graciously reviewed the man-
uscript in various forms and provided invaluable input. Sharon Wood-
house and everyone at Lake Claremont Press: thanks for taking that
gamble on me all those years ago. Two great bookstore owners: Allison
Platt of Bookies Paperbacks and More and Constance Shabazz of Books
Ink. Support your local independent bookstores, people! And, of course,

everyone at the Society of Midland Authors, America's best authors' association, bar none.

My wife, Cheryl Diddia-Bernstein, the strongest person I know.

My parents, Sheila and Gene Bernstein; and my in-laws, Nancy and Chuck Diddia: unfailingly supportive and understanding of my obsessions.

Jan Pagoria (my guardian angel) for all the usual reasons.

Above all, my heartfelt admiration and thanks to the witnesses and survivors of May 18, 1927: Harold Burnett, Willis Cressman, Lee Mast, and Josephine Cushman Vail. You have been so generous with your memories. Words cannot convey my gratitude for your faith in me. You have taught me so much about the unshakable resiliency of the human spirit. There is a balm in Gilead.

NOTES

PROLOGUE

1. Willis Cressman, interview with the author, June 1, 2007.

2. Josephine Cushman Vail, interview with the author, June 3, 2007.

3. "Virginia Tech Massacre," Wikipedia, http://en.wikipedia.org/wiki/Virginia_tech_shooting (accessed January 5, 2007).

4. Cressman interview.

5. Vail interview.

6. "Amish School Shooting," Wikipedia, http://en.wikipedia.org/wiki/Amish_school_shooting#Other_contemporary_school_shootings (accessed February 9, 2007).

CHAPTER 1

1. Harold Burnett, *History of Bath Charter Township, 1826–1976* (Bath: Harold B. Burnett, 1978), 1.

2. Ibid., 15.

3. Ibid., 18.

4. Ibid., 20.

5. Ibid., 21.

6. Gene Wilkins, *My Scrapbook on the Bath School Bombing of May 18, 1927* (Bath: Timber Wolf, 2002), 4.

7. Gene Wilkins, *Reflections of Bath, Michigan: Historical Look at the Bath/Park Lake Area through the Lens of a Camera* (Bath: Timber Wolf, 2005), 1.

8. Ibid., 4.

9. Ibid., 23–25.

10. Ibid., 5.

11. Ibid., 5.

12. "Thomas Edison," Wikipedia, http://en.wikipedia.org/wiki/Thomas_Edison#Electric_light (accessed March 12, 2007).

13. Burnett, *History of Bath Charter Township*, 112.

14. Ibid., 114.

15. Ibid., 131–38.

16. Ibid., 138.

17. "Dynamite," Wikipedia, http://en.wikipedia.org/wiki/Dynamite (accessed June 5, 2007).

18. "Pyrotol," Answers.com, http://www.answers.com/topic/pyrotol (accessed June 5, 2007).

19. Cressman interview.

CHAPTER 2

1. Vail interview.

2. "In the Matter of the Inquest as to the Cause of Death of Emery E. Huyck, Deceased," May 25, 1927, 182.

3. Florence Lowe Platt, interview with the author, May 19, 2007.

4. M. J. Ellsworth, *The Bath School Disaster* (Bath: M. J. Ellsworth, [1927] 2001), 26.

5. Grant Parker, *Mayday: The History of a Village Holocaust* (Perry, MI: Parker Press, 1980), 195.

6. Parker, *Mayday*, 196.

7. Ibid.

8. Ibid.

9. "Kehoe as Boy Made Electrical Devices," *Lansing State Journal*, May 20, 1927.

10. Ibid.

11. Parker, *Mayday*, 196.

12. Ibid., 198.

13. Ibid., 200.

14. Ibid., 199.

15. Ibid., 197.

16. Ibid., 203.

17. Ibid., 201.

18. Ibid., 203.

19. Ibid.

20. Ellsworth, *The Bath School Disaster*, 26.

21. "Kehoe Knew Few as Friend," *Lansing State Journal*, May 19, 1927.

22. Parker, *Mayday*, 204.

23. Ibid.

24. Ibid.

25. Ibid.

26. Ibid., 205–6.

27. Ellsworth, *The Bath School Disaster*, 28.

28. Parker, *Mayday*, 206
29. Ellsworth, *The Bath School Disaster*, 28.
30. Parker, *Mayday*, 206–7.
31. Ibid.
32. Ellsworth, *The Bath School Disaster*, 28.
33. Parker, *Mayday*, 26.
34. Ibid., 25.
35. Ibid., 208.
36. Ibid., 211.
37. Ellsworth, *The Bath School Disaster*, 26.
38. Ibid., 29.
39. Parker, *Mayday*, 25.
40. "In the Matter of the Inquest," 200.
41. Ellsworth, *The Bath School Disaster*, 29.
42. Ibid., 29–30.

CHAPTER 3

1. Laurence Bergreen, *Capone: The Man and the Era* (New York: Touchstone, 1994), 176–77.
2. Ibid., 162–67.
3. Ibid., 78.
4. Lee Mast, interview with the author, October 7, 2005.
5. Ibid.
6. Harold Burnett, interview with the author, November 18, 2007.
7. Wilkins, *Reflections of Bath*, 70.
8. Parker, *Mayday*, 3.
9. "Friday Afternoon Club," handout, undated.

CHAPTER 4

1. Ellsworth, *The Bath School Disaster*, 30.
2. Ibid.
3. Ibid.
4. "In the Matter of the Inquest," 124.
5. Ibid., 55.
6. Ellsworth, *The Bath School Disaster*, 31.
7. Parker, *Mayday*, 3.
8. Ellsworth, *The Bath School Disaster*, 35.
9. "In the Matter of the Inquest," 60.
10. Ibid., 181.
11. Ellsworth, *The Bath School Disaster*, 30.
12. Patti Seehase, interview with the author, June 2, 2007.
13. Ellsworth, *The Bath School Disaster*, 30.

CHAPTER 5

1. Burnett, *History of Bath Charter Township*, 161–62.
2. Ibid., 162.

3. Ibid., 162–64.

4. Ibid., 171.

5. Parker, *Mayday,* 10.

6. Ellsworth, *The Bath School Disaster,* 4.

7. Ibid., 5.

8. Wilkins, *My Scrapbook,* 11.

9. Parker, *Mayday,* 12.

10. Ellsworth, *The Bath School Disaster,* 36.

11. "Bath School Head Given Final Rites," *Lansing State Journal,* May 23, 1927.

12. Parker, *Mayday,* 13–14.

13. Ibid., 14.

14. Ibid., 18.

15. Cressman interview.

16. Burnett, *History of Bath Charter Township,* 199.

17. Ibid.

18. Parker, *Mayday,* 18–19.

19. Ibid., 21.

20. Ibid., 28.

21. Parker, *Mayday,* 30.

22. Ellsworth, *The Bath School Disaster,* 38.

23. Parker, *Mayday,* 33–37.

24. Ellsworth, *The Bath School Disaster,* 39.

25. Parker, *Mayday,* 38.

26. Ellsworth, *The Bath School Disaster,* 38.

27. Parker, *Mayday,* 82.

28. Ibid., 51.

29. "Assorted Quotes and Notes in Honor of Our Nation's Independence Day," Vision Forum, http://www.visionforum.com/hottopics/articles/2005-07-01_001.aspx (accessed August 1, 2007).

30. "In the Matter of the Inquest," 148–49.

31. Ellsworth, *The Bath School Disaster,* 31.

32. Parker, *Mayday,* 32–36.

33. Ibid., 44–45.

34. "In the Matter of the Inquest," 130–31.

35. Parker, *Mayday,* 51–57.

36. Ibid., 58–60.

37. Ellsworth, *The Bath School Disaster,* 29.

38. Parker, *Mayday,* 225.

39. Ellsworth, *The Bath School Disaster,* 39.

40. "In the Matter of the Inquest," 58.

41. Ibid., 64.

42. Ibid., 60–62.

43. Ibid., 60.

44. Parker, *Mayday,* 60.

45. "In the Matter of the Inquest," 146.

46. Ibid.

47. "Kehoe Knew Few as Friend," *Lansing State Journal,* May 19, 1927.

48. "In the Matter of the Inquest," 22–23.

CHAPTER 6

1. "In the Matter of the Inquest," 202–3.
2. Parker, *Mayday,* 43.
3. "In the Matter of the Inquest," 202.
4. Ibid., 205–6.
5. Ibid., 202–3.
6. "Bomber's Wife Is Found Slain, 44 Dead in Dynamite Tragedy," *Chicago Daily Journal,* May 19, 1927.
   7. Ellsworth, *The Bath School Disaster,* 31.
   8. Ibid., 35–36.
   9. Ibid., 36.
10. "Former Farm Bureau Mgr., Bath People Describe Andrew Kehoe," *Clinton County Republican-News,* May 26, 1927.
  11. "In the Matter of the Inquest," 343.
  12. M. S. Sweet, "Bath," *Lansing Capital Times,* December 31, 1926.
  13. "The Weather," *Lansing State Journal,* December 31, 1926.
  14. "In the Matter of the Inquest," 63–64.
  15. Ibid., 203.
  16. Ibid., 203–4.
  17. "M.S.C. Graduate, Teacher at Bath School Has Thrilling Memories," *Lansing State Journal,* May 21, 1927.
  18. Parker, *Mayday,* 50.
  19. "In the Matter of the Inquest," 26.
  20. Ibid., 270–75.
  21. Ibid., 185–86.
  22. Ibid., 343.
  23. Ibid., 20–21.
  24. Ibid., 132.
  25. Ellsworth, *The Bath School Disaster,* 32–33.
  26. *Lansing State Journal,* May 18, 1927.
  27. "In the Matter of the Inquest," 172.
  28. Ellsworth, *The Bath School Disaster,* 31–32.
  29. Parker, *Mayday,* 97.
  30. Ibid.
  31. "In the Matter of the Inquest," 182–83.
  32. Parker, *Mayday,* 98–99.
  33. "In the Matter of the Inquest," 173.
  34. Ibid., 136.
  35. "Kehoe Advised School Picnic 'Right Away,'" *Lansing State Journal,* May 19, 1927.
  36. "In the Matter of the Inquest," 186.
  37. Ibid., 209.
  38. *Clinton County Republican-News,* May 26, 1927.
  39. "The Making of Modern Michigan," http://archive.lib.msu.edu/MMM/JG/04/a/JG04a001.htm (accessed June 1, 2008).
  40. Ibid.
  41. "In the Matter of the Inquest," 320–21.

CHAPTER 7

1. "In the Matter of the Inquest," 25.
2. Burnett interview.
3. "In the Matter of the Inquest," 25.
4. "Records Fill Mystery Box," *Lansing State Journal*, May 19, 1927.
5. "In the Matter of the Inquest," 7–8.
6. Ellsworth, *The Bath School Disaster*, 69.
7. Vail interview.
8. "Reunion Stirs Memories of Bath Blast, Its Victims," *Detroit Free Press*, June 4, 1985.
9. Ellsworth, *The Bath School Disaster*, 64.
10. Ibid., 75.
11. "In the Matter of the Inquest," 40–41.
12. Ibid., 163–64.
13. Mast interview.
14. Ellsworth, *The Bath School Disaster*, 60.
15. Cressman interview.
16. Vail interview.
17. Wilkins, *My Scrapbook*, 46.
18. "In the Matter of the Inquest," 174.
19. Ibid., 52.
20. "Maniac Bomber's Wife among His 43 Victims," *Youngstown Telegraph*, May 19, 1927.
21. *Youngstown Telegraph*, "School Picnic Day In Bath one of Tragedy and Sorrow," May 19, 1927.
22. Ibid.
23. Parker, *Mayday*, 110.
24. "In the Matter of the Inquest," 153.
25. Ibid., 148.
26. Ibid., 164.
27. "School Head's Labor Wrecked," *Lansing State Journal*, May 18, 1927.
28. Wilkins, *My Scrapbook*, 47.
29. "Villagers Turn to Prayer after School Tragedy," *Toledo Blade*, May 19, 1927.
30. Cressman interview.
31. John McGonigal, interview with the author, May 19, 2007.
32. "In the Matter of the Inquest," 41.
33. *Lansing State Journal*, May 21, 1927.
34. Ellsworth, *The Bath School Disaster*, 104.
35. Vail interview.
36. "In the Matter of the Inquest," 11.
37. Ibid., 64–65.
38. Ibid., 293.
39. Ellsworth, *The Bath School Disaster*, 6.
40. "In the Matter of the Inquest," 246.
41. Ibid., 91–92.
42. Ibid., 137.
43. Ibid.
44. Ibid.

45. "School Dynamiter First Slew Wife," *New York Times*, May 20, 1927.

46. "Kehoe Sped to Destroy School as Neighbors Rallied to Assist Him," *Lansing State Journal*, May 19, 1927.

47. *New York Times*, May 20, 1927.

48. "In the Matter of the Inquest," 295.

49. Ibid., 143.

50. Ibid., 164.

51. Mast interview.

52. Parker, *Mayday*, 113.

53. "In the Matter of the Inquest," 154.

54. Ibid., 27.

55. Cressman interview.

56. Ellsworth, *The Bath School Disaster*, 84.

57. Jeff Seidel, "Life after Terrorism," *Detroit Free Press*, December 9, 2001.

58. Alice Loomis, interview with the author, December 7, 2007.

59. Ellsworth, *The Bath School Disaster*, 127.

60. "In the Matter of the Inquest," 92–95.

61. "Teacher, Pinned under Debris with Dead Boy, Has Prayers Answered," *Lansing State Journal*, May 20, 1927.

62. Wilkins, *My Scrapbook*, 50.

63. Chris Christoff, "2 Children of '27 Tragedy Say Crash Revives Suffering," *Detroit Free Press*, August 26, 1987.

64. Raymond Eschtruth, "May 18, 1927: The Way I Remember It," undated memoir.

65. Margrete Daney, "Funeral Dirges Sound as Echo of Maniac's Revenge," *Toledo Blade*, May 21, 1927.

66. Gene Wilkins, interview with the author, November 11, 2006.

67. Gerald G. Granger, "Frantic Mothers Search Line at Morgue for Own Children," *Lansing State Journal*, May 18, 1927.

68. *Lansing State Journal*, May 21, 1927.

69. Parker, *Mayday*, 116.

70. Ibid.

71. "Hint Accomplice in School Blast," *Chicago Daily News*, May 19, 1927.

72. Ellsworth, *The Bath School Disaster*, 7.

73. Wilkins, *My Scrapbook*, 47.

74. "In the Matter of the Inquest," 12.

75. "Lansing Rallies to Aid of Stricken Neighbor Town," *Lansing State Journal*, May 18, 1927.

76. Ibid.

77. Ibid.

78. "In the Matter of the Inquest," 65.

79. Ibid., 241.

80. Ibid., 65.

81. Ellsworth, *The Bath School Disaster*, 7.

82. Parker, *Mayday*, 119.

83. "In the Matter of the Inquest," 67.

84. Wilkins, *My Scrapbook*, 45.

85. "In the Matter of the Inquest," 213.

86. Eschtruth, "May 18, 1927."

87. "In the Matter of the Inquest," 233–34.

88. Ibid., 213.

89. Ellsworth, *The Bath School Disaster,* 21.

90. "In the Matter of the Inquest," 313–14.

91. Ibid., 33–34.

92. George Edward McConnell, interview with the author, September 28, 2005.

93. "In the Matter of the Inquest," 314.

94. Ellsworth, *The Bath School Disaster,* 74–75.

95. Ibid., 213.

96. Ibid., 156.

97. Ibid., 192.

98. Wilkins, *My Scrapbook,* 44.

99. "In the Matter of the Inquest," 34.

100. *Youngstown Telegraph,* May 19, 1927.

101. McConnell interview.

102. *New York Times,* May 20, 1927.

103. Eschtruth, "May 18, 1927."

104. Wilkins, *My Scrapbook,* 45.

105. "In the Matter of the Inquest," 14.

106. Vail interview.

107. *Lansing State Journal,* May 19, 1927.

108. Burnett interview.

109. Ellsworth, *The Bath School Disaster,* 67.

110. Ibid., 55.

111. Ibid., 127.

112. Ibid., 72.

113. Ibid., 104.

114. Ibid., 87.

115. "In the Matter of the Inquest," 30.

116. Ellsworth, *The Bath School Disaster,* 49.

117. *Clinton County Republican-News,* May 26, 1927.

118. "In the Matter of the Inquest," 30.

119. Ibid., 43.

120. Ibid.

CHAPTER 8

1. *Lansing State Journal,* May 18, 1927.

2. Wilkins, *My Scrapbook,* 47.

3. Vail interview.

4. Loomis interview.

5. *Youngstown Telegraph,* "Maniac Bomber's Wife Among Victims," May 19, 1927.

6. Parker, *Mayday,* 121.

7. Ellsworth, *The Bath School Disaster,* 15.

8. "In the Matter of the Inquest," 215.

9. *Chicago Daily News,* May 19, 1927.

10. Eschtruth, "May 18, 1927."

11. Ibid.

12. Wilkins, *My Scrapbook,* 51.

13. Ibid., 58–61.

14. *Detroit Free Press,* December 9, 2001.

15. *Toledo Blade,* May 19, 1927.

16. *Youngstown Telegraph,* "Maniac Bomber's Wife Among Victims," May 19, 1927.

17. McConnell interview.

18. *Toledo Blade,* May 19, 1927.

19. Colleen Cason, "Before Columbine: Oak View Man Witnessed Day 72 Years Ago When Terror Reigned at Schoolhouse," *Ventura County Star,* January 16, 2000.

20. Parker, *Mayday,* 134.

21. *Lansing State Journal,* May 19, 1927.

22. Parker, *Mayday,* 135.

23. "In the Matter of the Inquest," 213.

24. Burnett interview.

25. Charles E. Ahrens, "Day of School Picnic Opens Tragically," *Erie Daily Times,* May 19, 1927.

26. Parker, *Mayday,* 131.

27. "In the Matter of the Inquest," 14.

28. *Lansing State Journal,* May 20, 1927.

29. Ibid., 330.

30. Ibid., 329–31.

31. *Chicago Daily News,* May 19, 1927.

32. Vail interview.

33. Parker, *Mayday,* 133.

34. Wilkins, *My Scrapbook,* 55.

35. *Detroit Free Press,* December 9, 2001.

36. Parker, *Mayday,* 130.

37. Ibid.

38. "In the Matter of the Inquest," 332–38.

39. Ibid., 343.

40. James Doherty, "Call on State to Help School Tragedy Village," *Chicago Daily Tribune,* May 20, 1927.

41. Dean Sweet Jr., interview with the author, April 4, 2008.

42. "In the Matter of the Inquest," 332.

43. *Lansing State Journal,* May 19, 1927.

44. *Chicago Daily Tribune,* May 20, 1927.

45. "Disaster Seen to Spur Drive," *Lansing State Journal,* May 18, 1927.

46. "In the Matter of the Inquest," 208.

47. *Lansing State Journal,* May 20, 1927.

48. Parker, *Mayday,* 133.

49. "Press Room Set Up in Tiny Woodshed," *Lansing State Journal,* May 19, 1927.

50. Parker, *Mayday,* 133.

51. Burnett interview.

52. *Lansing State Journal,* May 20, 1927.

53. "Blast Photos Rushed by Air for *Herald-Examiner* Scoop," *Chicago Herald-Examiner,* May 19, 1927.

54. "Planes Carry Blast Films to Eastern Movie Houses," *Lansing State Journal,* May 20, 1927.

55. "Airplane and Automobile Used by *Blade* to Cover School Blast," *Toledo Blade,* May 19, 1927.

56. Parker, *Mayday,* 136–38.

57. Ellsworth, *The Bath School Disaster,* 127.

58. "In the Matter of the Inquest," 208–11.

59. Vail interview.

60. *Chicago Daily News,* May 19, 1927.

61. Dr. R. G. Curtis Jr., interview with the author, December 9, 2007.

62. *Lansing State Journal,* May 18, 1927.

63. "In the Matter of the Inquest," 215.

64. Vail interview.

65. "Fiend Dynamites Bath School, 44 Die," *Clinton County Republican-News,* May 19, 1927.

66. Vail interview.

67. Ellsworth, *The Bath School Disaster,* 67.

68. *Lansing State Journal,* May 18, 1927.

69. Vail interview.

70. *Lansing State Journal,* May 20, 1927.

71. Ibid., 40–41.

72. *Lansing State Journal,* May 19, 1927.

73. Vail interview.

74. *Clinton County Republican-News,* May 19, 1927.

75. Loomis interview.

CHAPTER 9

1. *Toledo Blade,* May 19, 1927.

2. Ibid.

3. Ibid.

4. *Chicago Herald-Examiner,* May 19, 1927.

5. *Lansing State Journal,* May 19, 1927.

6. Ibid.

7. Ibid.

8. Ibid.

9. "Disaster Fund Grows Hourly," *Lansing State Journal,* May 21, 1927.

10. Ibid.

11. "Over $7,300 in Bath Aid Fund," *Lansing State Journal,* May 26, 1927.

12. "Ingham Towns Plan Bath Benefit Shows," *Lansing State Journal,* May 23, 1927.

13. *Lansing State Journal,* May 21, 1927.

14. Ibid.

15. "James J. Couzens," Wikipedia, http://en.wikipedia.org/wiki/James_Couzens (accessed August 7, 2007).

16. Parker, *Mayday,* 175.

17. "James J. Couzens."

18. *Lansing State Journal,* May 20, 1927.

19. Parker, *Mayday,* 172.

20. *Lansing State Journal,* May 21, 1927.

21. Parker, *Mayday,* 176.

22. *Lansing State Journal,* May 19, 1927.

23. Ibid.

24. *Toledo Blade,* May 21, 1927.

25. *Lansing State Journal,* May 19, 1927.

26. Ellsworth, *The Bath School Disaster,* 26.

27. *Lansing State Journal,* May 20, 1927.

28. *Ventura County Star,* January 16, 2000.

29. "In the Matter of the Inquest," 219–22.

30. *Lansing State Journal,* May 23, 1927.

31. Ibid.

32. *Lansing State Journal,* May 20, 1927.

33. Ibid.

34. *Clinton County Republican-News,* May 26, 1927.

35. Ibid.

CHAPTER 10

1. Patti Seehase interview.

2. Ted Christie, "Begin Sift of Bath Disaster," *Lansing State Journal,* May 19, 1927.

3. *Toledo Blade,* May 21, 1927.

4. "The Making of Modern Michigan," http://archive.lib.msu.edu/MMM/JG/04/a/JG04a001.htm (accessed June 1, 2008).

5. *Lansing State Journal,* May 20, 1927.

6. Wilkins interview.

7. *Lansing State Journal,* May 20, 1927.

8. "Stricken Town Silent at Biers of 11 Blast Victims," *Chicago Herald-Examiner,* May 21, 1927.

9. Ibid.

10. Ellsworth, *The Bath School Disaster,* 104.

11. *Lansing State Journal,* May 23, 1927.

12. *Toledo Blade,* May 21, 1927.

13. "The Making of Modern Michigan" http://archive.lib.msu.edu/MMM/JG/04/g/JG04g001.html (accessed June 1, 2008).

14. David Seehase, interview with the author, May 17, 2008.

15. Vail interview.

16. Ibid.

17. Ibid.

18. *Lansing State Journal,* May 20, 1927.

19. "Bath School Head Given Final Rites," *Lansing State Journal,* May 23, 1927.

20. *Clinton County Republican-News,* May 26, 1927.

21. *Erie Daily Times,* May 21, 1927.

22. *Lansing State Journal,* May 20, 1927.

23. Parker, *Mayday,* 152.

24. *Lansing State Journal,* May 23, 1927.

25. Ibid.

26. *Clinton County Republican-News,* May 26, 1927.

27. *Clinton County Republican-News,* May 26, 1927.

28. Parker, *Mayday,* 156.

29. "Minutes of Bath School Board Meeting," May 2, 1927.

30. Parker, *Mayday,* 156.

31. "Minutes of Bath School Board Meeting," May 20, 1927.

32. *Lansing State Journal,* May 21, 1927.

33. Ibid.

34. Ibid.

35. Ibid.

36. "Minutes of Bath School Board Meeting," May 20, 1927.

CHAPTER 11

Superintendent Huyck's first name is properly spelled "Emory" but was misspelled as "Emery" in the official inquest.

1. *Lansing State Journal,* May 19, 1927.

2. Ibid.

3. Parker, *Mayday,* 161.

4. Ibid.

5. *Lansing State Journal,* May 19, 1927.

6. *Lansing State Journal,* May 20, 1927.

7. "In the Matter of the Inquest," 95.

8. Ibid., 347.

9. "Inquest to as Cause of Death, State of Michigan, County of Clinton, May 25, 1927," 2.

10. "In the Matter of the Inquest," 202–3.

11. Lisa W. Foderaro, "New York Has Long Been a Capital of Psychotherapy: How Have the Options Changed?" *New York Times,* September 10, 1995.

12. "Closing Arguments of Clarence Darrow," Leopold and Loeb.com, http://www.leopoldandloeb.com/closingdefense.html (accessed October 10, 2007).

13. *Lansing State Journal,* May 23, 1927.

14. David D. Hare, *Without Conscience: The Disturbing World of the Psychopaths among Us* (New York and London: Guilford Press, 1999), 5.

15. "In the Matter of the Inquest," 349.

CHAPTER 12

1. Loomis interview.

2. "Bath Crime Suggests New Noun, New Verb," *Lansing State Journal,* May 27, 1927.

3. *Clinton County Republican-News,* May 26, 1927.

4. "In the Matter of the Inquest," 105.

5. "Defends Kehoe before Crowd," *Clinton County Republican-News,* June 23, 1927.

6. Vail interview.

7. Parker, *Mayday*, 182.

8. Vail interview.

9. "Minutes of Bath School Board Meeting," June 10, 1927.

10. Curtis interview.

11. *Clinton County Republican-News*, May 26, 1927.

12. Ibid.

13. Fredrick Lewis Allen, *Only Yesterday: An Informal History of the 1920s* (New York: Bantam, 1946), 84.

14. "Hugo Black," Wikipedia, http://en.wikipedia.org/wiki/Hugo_Black (accessed October 5, 2007).

15. Parker, *Mayday*, 120.

16. "Roman Catholic Dynamites Bath Public Schools," undated broadsheet.

17. Parker, *Mayday*, 177.

18. "Bath Accepts Couzens Offer," *Lansing State Journal*, June 24, 1927.

19. *Detroit Free Press*, December 9, 2001.

20. Ibid.

21. United Press International, "Five More Dying in School Blast," *Youngstown Vindicator*, May 20, 1927.

22. Cressman interview.

23. Ellsworth, *The Bath School Disaster*, 117.

24. *Detroit Free Press*, August 26, 1987.

25. Ellsworth, *The Bath School Disaster*, 104–5.

26. Ellsworth, *The Bath School Disaster*, 3.

27. Burnett interview.

28. Ellsworth, *The Bath School Disaster*, 74–75.

29. *Detroit Free Press*, December 9, 2001.

30. Wilkins, *My Scrapbook*, 51.

31. Vail interview.

32. Mast interview.

33. *Detroit Free Press*, August 26, 1987.

34. *Lansing State Journal*, May 27, 1927.

35. Ibid.

CHAPTER 13

1. Wilkins, *My Scrapbook*, 56.

2. "Bath School Ruins Reveal More of Plot," *Lansing State Journal*, July 21, 1927.

3. "School Yields More Dynamite," *Lansing State Journal*, July 18, 1927.

4. Wilkins, *My Scrapbook*, 38.

5. Cressman interview.

6. Vail interview.

7. Burnett, *History of Bath Charter Township*, 219.

8. Ibid.

9. Frank Pritchard, "Valley of Tears made Mecca of Curious during Funerals," *Lansing State Journal*, May 23, 1927.

10. Burnett, *History of Bath Charter Township*, 220.

11. Patti Seehase interview.

12. Ibid.

13. Wilkins, *Reflections of Bath,* 95.

14. Loomis interview.

15. Wilkins, *My Scrapbook,* 63.

16. David Seehase interview, May 17, 2008.

17. *Detroit Free Press,* December 9, 2001.

18. *Detroit Free Press,* August 26, 1987.

19. Patti Seehase interview.

20. Ibid.

21. Julie Teed, interview with the author, February 15, 2007.

22. Wayne Loomis, interview with the author, December 7, 2007.

23. Patti Seehase interview.

24. Burnett, *History of Bath Charter Township,* 226–27.

25. Parker, *Mayday,* 226.

26. Burnett, *History of Bath Charter Township,* 226–27.

27. *Detroit Free Press,* December 9, 2001.

28. Teed interview.

29. Roger Friend, interview with the author, September 28, 2005.

30. Burnett, *History of Bath Charter Township,* 224.

31. Ibid., 225.

32. Ibid., 222.

33. Parker, *Mayday,* 239.

34. Burnett, *History of Bath Charter Township,* 221.

35. Patti Seehase interview.

36. Loomis interview.

37. Wilkins interview.

38. *Detroit Free Press,* December 9, 2001.

39. Ibid.

40. Ibid.

41. McConnell interview.

42. "School Shootings," Wikipedia, http://en.wikipedia.org/wiki/School _shootings (accessed August 17, 2007).

43. "Bath School Disaster," http://freepages.history.rootsweb.ancestry .com/~bauerle/disaster.htm (accessed January 5, 2006).

44. Parker, *Mayday,* 231.

45. Nancy Welch Spagnulo, interview with the author, May 18, 2007.

46. Vail interview.

47. Heather Chadwick, interview with the author, May 22, 2007.

48. Ibid.

SELECTIVE BIBLIOGRAPHY

BOOKS

Allen, Frederick Lewis. *Only Yesterday: An Informal History of the Nineteen-twenties.* Bantam Books, 1946.

Burnett, Harold B. *History of Bath Charter Township: 1826–1976.* 1978.

Ellsworth, M. J. *The Bath School Disaster.* 1927.

Parker, Grant. *Mayday: The History of a Village Holocaust.* Parker Press, 1980.

Hare, Robert D. *Without Conscience: The Disturbing World of the Psychopaths among Us.* Pocket Books, 1995.

Wilkins, Gene H. *My Scrapbook on the Bath School Bombing of May 18th, 1927.* Timber Wolf, 2002.

Wilkins, Gene H. *Reflections of Bath, Michigan: A Historical Look at the Bath/Park Lake Area through the Lens of a Camera.* Timber Wolf, 2005.

NEWSPAPERS

Chicago Daily News
Chicago Daily Tribune
Chicago Herald and Examiner
Clinton County Republican News
Detroit Free Press
Erie Daily Times
Lansing State Journal
New York Times

Toledo Blade
Youngstown Telegraph
Youngstown Vindicator

PUBLIC DOCUMENTS

"In the Matter of the Inquest as to the Cause of Death of Emery E. Huyck, Deceased." May 25, 1927.

INTERVIEWS

Burnett, Harold. November 18, 2006.
Chadwick, Heather. May 22, 2007.
Cressman, Willis. June 1, 2007.
Curtis, R. G. December 9, 2007.
Friend, Roger. September 28, 2005.
Loomis, Alice. December 7, 2007.
Loomis, Wayne. December 7, 2007.
Mast, Lee. October 7, 2005.
McConnell, George Edward. September 28, 2005.
McGonigal, John. May 19, 2007.
Platt, Florence Lowe. May 19, 2007.
Seehase, Patti. June 2, 2007.
Teed, Julie. June 2, 2007.
Vail, Josephine Cushman. May 22, 2007.
Wilkins, Gene H. October 15, 2005.

WEB SITES

"The Bath School Disaster." http://freepages.history.rootsweb.ancestry.com/~bauerle/disaster.htm.
"Information about the Bath School Disaster." http://daggy.name/tbsd.